A Practical Legal Guide for Tourists and Business Travelers

Thailand

By Michael L. Moore Esq.

DEDICATION

This book is dedicated to the memory of my late older brother, Kenneth Lee Moore, whose tragic murder at 15 years of age inspired me to write this series of books.

This book is also dedicated to my parents, John Henry Moore, and Edna Mae Moore, whose tremendous parenting skills kept me focused on the important things in life: being reverent, getting educated, and prioritizing family.

Finally, this book is dedicated to my beautiful family, my wife Royellen, my son AJ, and my daughter Karla. They inspire me every single day to be kind, patient, and compassionate.

IN LOVING MEMORY OF:

Belinda Joyce Moore Moss—my beautiful and wonderful sister, who supported me in every positive thing that I ever attempted to do.

Michael Eugene Baker—my dedicated and loyal friend and brother, who always wanted the very best for me.

Sylvia Joyce Hill—my eldest sister, who had a beautiful spirit and was like a second mother to me.

LAW OF THE LAND ®

PUBLISHING for Tourists & Business Travelers

Travel smart. Stay legal. Stay safe.®

From local laws to medical guides we've got you covered world wide
in one digital platform.

Travel Safe Anywhere
3 MONTHS FREE TRIAL

SCAN QR code
for more info

PREFACE

My introduction to the justice system came when I was only 10 years old. My 15-year-old brother was murdered with a butcher knife by a 19-year-old in a simple argument over a torn shirt. I was devastated by his death and sought retribution for his fate that never came. The woman was initially charged with second degree murder, but after plea negotiations, she was convicted of manslaughter and sentenced to only five years in a youthful offender school and ordered to undergo psychiatric care. That was it. Nothing more. The judicial system had run its course.

My family knew nothing about the justice system, and we did not have the tools to advocate for ourselves. No one provided us with a written source to reference for guidance through this process. There was no easily accessible, easy to understand, definitive source to educate ourselves about the legal system that we suddenly and unexpectedly found ourselves immersed in after being victimized by such a violent criminal act.

As I got older, finished college, law school, and ultimately started practicing law, it became clear to me that most people are not knowledgeable about the law or how the judicial process works. If most people are uninformed here in the United States regarding the law and the legal process, how would they fare when in other countries? I realized that tourists and businesspeople who travel internationally needed access to information on how to navigate the legal system in other countries!

For many years, there has been considerable media attention focused on international travelers experiencing legal difficulties while traveling abroad. Most of these news stories gained attention in the United States and abroad because they involved American citizens facing punishment that was considered "unconventional" and "harsh" by United States' legal standards. I recall a news story in 1994 regarding Michael Fay, a young American male, who had broken the law in Singapore. He was convicted and sentenced to be caned and or whipped publicly. While the United States Government weighed in on the inappropriate and cruel nature of the punishment, the young American was beaten because he had been convicted under Singapore law.

Similarly, in recent years, international news stories have garnered headlines regarding foreign travelers and their issues with the laws of countries that were not their own. Amanda Knox, an American woman, was accused of murdering her roommate in Italy in 2007 and spent almost four years in an Italian prison before being definitively acquitted by the Supreme Court of Cassatio. Kenneth Bae, an American citizen, was arrested in North Korea in 2012 and was convicted for hostile acts against the communist country. He was sentenced to 15 years hard labor but was released in 2014 after efforts by the U.S. State Department. More recently, United States Basketball Star, Brittany Griner was arrested in February 2022 at a Moscow airport on drug-related charges and detained for nearly 10 months, spending much of that time in prison. Her plight unfolded at the same time Russia invaded Ukraine and further heightened tensions between Russia and the United States, ending only after she was freed in exchange for a notorious Russian arms dealer.

It was in 1994 that another personal tragic event occurred that finally inspired me to write these series of books. A dear friend and also client of mine was brutally murdered while on his second honeymoon in Jamaica. News of his murder shocked me and our local community. The legal hurdles his family had to overcome to see that justice was properly dispensed far away from home, in another country, with an entirely different set of criminal procedural rules and laws, was difficult to navigate.

As I was my friend's attorney at the time of his death, his family asked that I act as their "legal liaison" to the Jamaican Prosecutor's Office and to the Jamaican Police Department. I participated in multiple police interviews with my client's widow because she was the primary witness to his murder. As a former prosecuting attorney, I was also allowed by the Court, as a professional courtesy, to sit at the prosecutor's table to consult with the prosecuting attorney during trial. What I observed about the Jamaican trial process from a front row seat was compelling enough to cause me to seriously consider educating the "world" regarding what to expect and how to act appropriately when faced with legal issues while traveling abroad.

One of the realities in life is that, regardless of what country you are in, it is never a pleasant experience to run afoul of the law and be forced to accept that someone else will be making a decision about your pecuniary, proprietary, or penal interests (your money, your property, or your freedom).

It is important to know what the laws are, how they apply to you, and how to navigate the legal system if you are charged with a crime. It is also very helpful to know what resources are available to you if you are the victim of a criminal act. At the end of the day, an "ounce of prevention is worth a pound of cure," so the more knowledge you have, the more ammunition you possess, and the more likely you will have a positive outcome.

If you are traveling to Thailand, the first thing you should pack is a copy of this book! The helpful information and tips contained in this volume will provide a great starting point for knowing what to do (and not to do!) when you arrive at your destination and will help ensure that you have a wonderful vacation or business trip unmarred by tangles with the law.

TABLE OF CONTENTS

INTRODUCTION

INTRODUCTION

As a practicing attorney for over 34 years, I have encountered numerous clients who travel often, but are unaware of the laws of the land they are traveling to.

Therefore, many years ago, I decided to write a series of books that would explain the laws of specific countries. My focus was to explain the laws that may affect travelers in a straightforward manner, without all of the legal language that is sometimes hard for even seasoned attorneys to understand.

About This Book

The aim of this book is simple. It provides you, the traveler, with a simple, easy to read book that will provide a basic legal guide that explains the law in the country that you are about to visit. It is not intended to educate you on ALL of the laws in a given country. The goal is to provide you with the details of the most common legal and safety issues faced by tourists and business travelers.

I have also provided context with background information on places not to visit, statistics on the country and prevention measures you should take to safeguard your legal and physical safety. Knowledge is a powerful thing and knowing how to stay out of trouble (or how to get out of it!) is important for everyone who travels.

This *Law of The Land/Thailand* book simply helps you become more informed about your legal rights, responsibilities, and obligations in a wide range of subject areas.

Last, but not least, this book does NOT purport to offer legal advice. It does, however, provide the information you need to stay safe, follow the law and navigate around legal difficulties. However, if you do face legal difficulties, the information in this book will provide you with a starting point for solving the problem and obtaining legal assistance should it be required.

Hypotheticals Used Throughout This Book

From time to time throughout this book, I will explain the law to readers by using hypothetical scenarios. These hypotheticals will be marked by an icon that will be explained in further detail as you read on.

How This Book is Organized

CHAPTER 1: **About Thailand.** This chapter will provide you with a brief overview about Thailand and its history. It also addresses Visa requirements, monetary advice, and the best times to visit.

CHAPTER 2: **Customs.** This chapter will provide information on what to expect when entering Thailand. It will also explain what restricted and prohibited items are when entering Thailand along with custom's regulations.

CHAPTER 3: **Crime in Thailand.** This chapter provides an overview of the history of crime in Thailand and steps that Thailand's officials have taken to curb the high rate of crime.

CHAPTER 4: **Criminal Law Violations.** This chapter will provide information on drug offenses, penalties, true events and questions and answers.

CHAPTER 5: **Alcohol-Related Offenses.** This chapter will provide key points regarding the sale, consumption, and regulations of alcohol use in Thailand.

CHAPTER 6: **Firearm & Ammunition Offenses.** This chapter will provide key points regarding the possession of firearms and ammunition in Thailand.

CHAPTER 7: **Prostitution.** This chapter provides an overview of the history of prostitution in Thailand, laws and penalties, prostitution practices, sex trafficking, sex tourism, health in Thailand, tips to avoid being hassled, a Law of the Land Hypothetical, and the current situation on prostitution in Thailand.

CHAPTER 8: **LGBTQ.** This chapter will provide information regarding the acceptance of LGBTQ people in Thailand and the laws surrounding homosexuality.

CHAPTER 9: **Sexually Motivated/Violent Crimes.** This chapter will provide an overview of sexually related crimes in Thailand.

CHAPTER 10: **Arrested in Thailand.** This chapter will provide information on what to do if you are arrested in Thailand.

CHAPTER 11: **Jails vs. Prisons: Conditions & Culture.** This chapter will provide information on the conditions and culture of Thailand's Jails and Prisons.

CHAPTER 12: **Helping a Friend or Relative Imprisoned in Thailand.** This chapter will provide information on how you can assist a friend or relative imprisoned in Thailand.

CHAPTER 13: **The Administration of Justice.** This chapter will provide information on Thailand's Legal System.

CHAPTER 14: **Crime Victim Assistance.** This chapter will provide information on crime victim assistance along with providing safety tips.

CHAPTER 15: **Police.** This chapter will provide information on Thailand's Police and how to report a crime.

CHAPTER 16: **How to Get Legal Help in Thailand.** This chapter will provide information regarding how to obtain legal assistance for travelers to Thailand.

CHAPTER 17: **Medical Facilities & Hospitals.** This chapter will provide information about how to obtain medical care while visiting Thailand.

CHAPTER 18: **Driving in Thailand.** This chapter will provide information on driving in Thailand, traffic rules, and road safety tips.

CHAPTER 19: **Nude Beaches & Clothing-Optional Resorts.** This chapter will provide an overview of nude beaches and clothing-optional resorts in Thailand, and the legality and safety of visiting nude beaches in Thailand.

CHAPTER 20: **Unusual Laws.** This chapter will provide information on some Unusual Laws in Thailand, and penalties and fines.

CHAPTER 21: **Traveling Safely.** This chapter will provide information on women traveling alone, crime prevention for families, safety notes for all travelers, and overall advice.

CHAPTER 22: **Tourist Taxation.** This chapter will provide information on taxes that tourists are required to pay in Thailand.

CHAPTER 23: **Long-Term Stays.** This chapter will provide an overview of the consequences for overstaying your visit to Thailand.

CHAPTER 24: **Civil Litigation.** This chapter will provide information about the civil litigation process in Thailand.

CHAPTER 25: **Other Things to Know.** This chapter will provide information on the harassment of tourists, travel and safety, and other practical tips.

CHAPTER 26: **Quick Reference Guide.** This chapter is a quick way to get information. It is a condensed version of the chapters in this book.

Emergency/Important Contact Numbers in Thailand

Useful Thai Phrases

Glossary

Icons Used in this Book

What do those pictures throughout the book mean? See below:

 WARNING: This icon flags information about things you should **avoid** while visiting Thailand. Heed the advice next to this icon to avoid legal perils.

 REMEMBER: This icon flags noteworthy information that you **shouldn't forget.**

 HELPFUL TIPS: This icon flags information that will help you when entering Thailand, relates to a legal situation, or refers to resources available while visiting Thailand.

 TECHNICAL INFORMATION: This icon flags technical aspects of the law. If you are faced with a legal problem, and you want to learn more about the law involved, this information can be helpful.

 **ADDITIONAL INFORMATION:** This icon points to the location of additional information available on the internet.

 **HYPOTHETICAL:** This icon points to hypothetical scenarios to illustrate possible legal problems and the outcome.

 **QUESTIONS:** This icon points to questions and answers throughout the book.

 **TRUE STORY:** This icon points to true events throughout the book.

Where to Go From Here

If you have a specific question about the law in Thailand as it relates to a particular area, just turn to the chapter that addresses that issue, or turn to the Quick Reference Guide. You can also read the book from cover to cover to obtain a more comprehensive understanding of Thailand's laws and resources available should you find yourself in a legal predicament while visiting.

 **Disclaimer:** While the recommendations in this book primarily address U.S. citizens, the information is relevant and applicable to citizens of any country.

CHAPTER 1
ABOUT THAILAND

ABOUT THAILAND

About Thailand

Thailand is located in **Southeast Asia** and shares borders with Myanmar to the northwest, Laos to the north and east, Cambodia to the southeast, and Malaysia to the south. It also has long coastlines along the Andaman Sea and the Gulf of Thailand, which give it access to beautiful beaches and a thriving maritime economy. The country covers approximately **198,120 square miles** (513,120 square kilometers), making it slightly smaller than France and slightly larger than Spain. As of 2023, Thailand has a population of **around 71 million people.** It is known globally for its tropical beaches, ornate temples, spicy cuisine, vibrant street markets, and friendly people. Thailand attracts millions of tourists each year for its cultural richness, affordability, and natural beauty, with top destinations including Bangkok, Chiang Mai, Phuket, and the Phi Phi Islands.

Thailand has a long and independent history that sets it apart from many other Southeast Asian nations. Formerly known as **Siam**, Thailand has never been colonized by a Western power, maintaining sovereignty while adapting to global shifts. Its history includes powerful ancient kingdoms such as Sukhothai, Ayutthaya, and Lanna. The Ayutthaya Kingdom was particularly influential until it fell to the Burmese in the 18th century. Afterward, the capital was moved to Bangkok by King Rama I in 1782, beginning the current Chakri Dynasty. In 1939, the country officially changed its name to Thailand, which means **"Land of the Free."** The country has experienced political ups and downs over the past century, including coups and shifts between military and civilian governments. However, it has maintained relative stability and continues to grow as a regional economic and cultural hub.

Bangkok, the capital of Thailand, is a bustling metropolis located in the central region along the Chao Phraya River. It is the country's largest city and serves as its **economic, political, and cultural center.** With a population exceeding 10 million, Bangkok is known for its skyscrapers, historic temples, vibrant street food culture, and dynamic nightlife. Major attractions include the **Grand Palace, Wat Phra Kaew** (Temple of the Emerald Buddha), **Wat Arun** (Temple of Dawn), and the sprawling **Chatuchak Weekend Market.** Bangkok is also home to modern shopping malls, rooftop bars, and luxury hotels, offering a mix of traditional Thai culture and contemporary urban life.

The people of Thailand, known as **Thais,** are widely recognized for their hospitality, warmth, and easygoing nature—Thailand is often referred to as the "Land of Smiles." Thai society places great value on **family, respect for elders,** and **community.** Social harmony is important, and personal behavior is guided by concepts like "saving face" and avoiding conflict. The country is ethnically diverse, with most citizens being ethnically Thai, but there are also large communities of Chinese Thais, Malays in the south, and various hill tribes in the north such as the Hmong, Karen, and Lahu. Despite regional differences, Thai people are united by their shared culture, national pride, and devotion to the monarchy.

The **official language** of Thailand is **Thai,** a tonal language with its own distinct script. It is spoken nationwide and used in government, media, and education. Several regional dialects also exist, including Isan in the northeast, Northern Thai, and Southern Thai. In areas with ethnic minorities, languages such as Hmong, Karen, and Malay are also spoken. English is widely taught in schools and is commonly used in tourist areas, though fluency levels vary. In urban centers like Bangkok, English is generally well-understood in hotels, restaurants, and transport services.

The most dominant religion in Thailand is **Buddhism,** practiced by **over 90 percent** of the population. Specifically, Theravāda Buddhism shapes much of Thai culture, values, and daily life. Monks are highly respected, and it is common for young men to spend time in a monastery as a rite of passage. Temples, known as "wats," are found throughout the country and play a central role in both religious and community life. Other religions are also practiced freely, including Islam (especially in the southern provinces), Christianity, Hinduism, and Sikhism. Thailand guarantees **religious freedom** and is **generally tolerant of different beliefs and practices.**

Thailand is widely considered an **affordable destination,** both for tourists and for those looking to live or stay long-term. Accommodation options range from simple hostels starting at around $10 to $15 USD per night, to mid-range hotels priced between $40 to $80 USD, and luxury resorts that can still be relatively affordable compared to Western countries, typically ranging from $100 to $250 USD per night depending on location and season. Food in Thailand is famously inexpensive and delicious. Street food meals often cost just $1 to $3 USD, while a full meal in a casual sit-down restaurant might be around $5 to $15 USD. High-end dining in Bangkok or resort areas may cost $30 USD or more, but still offers excellent value for the quality. Transportation is also low-cost and efficient. A ride on the BTS Skytrain in Bangkok costs about $0.50 to $1.50 USD, and intercity buses and trains offer budget-friendly travel options. Domestic flights between major cities often range from $25 to $80 USD. Entry to temples is usually free or under $5 USD, and guided tours typically cost between $20 and $60 USD. Overall, Thailand provides a high quality of life at a relatively low cost, making it attractive to travelers, retirees, and digital nomads alike.

Thailand, the Basics

How to Get There?

Thailand is easily accessible by air, with several international airports welcoming travelers from all over the world. The main international gateway is **Suvarnabhumi Airport (BKK)** in Bangkok, one of the busiest airports in Southeast Asia. This modern hub serves as the primary base for **Thai Airways**, the country's flagship carrier, as well as for other major airlines like Bangkok Airways and Thai VietJet. Another important airport is **Don Mueang International Airport (DMK)**, also located in Bangkok, which mainly handles low-cost carriers such as **AirAsia, Nok Air,** and **Scoot,** offering budget-friendly flights across Asia. In northern Thailand, **Chiang Mai International Airport (CNX)** connects travelers to regional and international destinations, while **Phuket International Airport (HKT)** in the south serves tourists heading to the country's famous beaches and islands. These airports host flights from global airlines including **Emirates, Qatar Airways, Lufthansa, EVA Air, Singapore Airlines,** and **Korean Air,** providing direct or one-stop service from cities in North America, Europe, Australia, and throughout Asia.

The cheapest time to fly to Thailand is typically during the **low season,** which runs from **May through early October,** coinciding with the rainy or monsoon season. While the weather can be unpredictable during this period, savvy travelers can save significantly on airfare and accommodations. Round-trip flights from the United States to Bangkok during the low season can often be found for **$700 to $900 USD,** compared to **$1,200 or more** during the peak months of **December to February.** Booking flights about **two to three months in advance** and flying midweek—especially on Tuesdays and Wednesdays—can also help lower costs. Budget airlines offer incredibly affordable fares for travel within Southeast Asia, with one-way flights from nearby countries like Vietnam, Malaysia, or Singapore to Thailand starting as low as **$30 to $70 USD** depending on the route and time of year.

When to Visit?

The best time to visit Thailand depends on your priorities—weather, crowds, or cultural experiences—but for most travelers, the ideal period is during the **cool and dry season from November to February.** This stretch offers comfortable daytime temperatures ranging from **75–88°F (24–31°C),** low humidity, and sunny skies, making it perfect for beach vacations, city exploration, and outdoor adventures. It's also the most popular time for tourists, especially around Christmas and New Year's, so expect higher prices and more crowded attractions. If you're looking to avoid the crowds while still enjoying fairly good weather, **March to**

early May can be a good option, although it gets much hotter—especially in inland cities like Bangkok and Chiang Mai, where temperatures can soar to **100°F (38°C)**. This time of year is great for diving in the Similan Islands or exploring the less-visited parts of northern Thailand.

The **low season**, from **May to October**, brings the rainy monsoon across much of the country. While downpours can be intense, they're often short-lived and usually occur in the late afternoon. This is also when Thailand is at its greenest and most lush. Plus, this period sees fewer tourists and **lower prices for accommodations and tours—sometimes up to 40% off regular rates**. It's also a great time for cultural travel and slow exploration.

Thailand is renowned for its vibrant festivals, and timing your visit around one can offer an unforgettable experience. One of the most iconic is **Songkran**, the Thai New Year celebrated in **mid-April**, where the entire country turns into a joyful water fight—especially wild in Chiang Mai and Bangkok. In **November**, the magical **Loy Krathong** and **Yi Peng** festivals light up the night with floating lanterns and candle-lit offerings on rivers and in the sky, especially stunning in Chiang Mai. Other notable events include the **Vegetarian Festival** in Phuket (usually in October), known for its colorful processions and intense rituals, and the **Rocket Festival** (Bun Bang Fai) in northeastern Thailand during **May**, which blends traditional music, dance, and homemade rocket launches to encourage rainfall.

Do I Need a Visa?

Whether you need a visa to enter Thailand depends on your nationality and the length of your stay. **Citizens of the United States, Canada, the United Kingdom, most EU countries, Australia**, and several others can enter Thailand **visa-free for up to 30 days when arriving by air**, and up to **15 days when arriving overland** from a neighboring country. This applies to tourism purposes only, and travelers must show proof of onward travel and sufficient funds for their stay. If you plan to stay longer, you can apply for a **Tourist Visa,** which typically allows for a **60-day stay** with the option to extend once for an additional 30 days at a Thai immigration office.

A single-entry Tourist Visa costs approximately **$40–$50 USD,** depending on your country of application, and must be obtained before arrival from a Thai consulate or embassy. If you're planning a longer stay or multiple entries into Thailand, the **Multiple-Entry Tourist Visa** is available and valid for 6 months (each visit up to 60 days), costing about **$150–$200 USD.**

Thailand also offers **visa on arrival** (VOA) for citizens of certain countries for a stay of up to 15 days, with a fee of **2,000 Thai Baht** (**around $55 USD**), payable in cash at the airport. For the most up-to-date and personalized visa requirements, it's always best to check with the Thai Embassy or Consulate in your home country before traveling.

How to Get Around

Getting around Thailand is generally easy, affordable, and offers a wide range of options for every type of traveler. In major cities like Bangkok and Chiang Mai, **taxis, tuk-tuks, and rideshare apps like Grab** (the Southeast Asian equivalent of Uber) are widely available and inexpensive. A short taxi or Grab ride across town typically costs **$2 to $5 USD,** while a tuk-tuk ride may cost **$3 to $7 USD,** depending on distance and your bargaining skills. In Bangkok, the **BTS Skytrain** and **MRT subway** are highly efficient ways to navigate the city, with fares ranging from **$0.50 to $1.50 USD per ride**—ideal for avoiding traffic and staying cool in the heat.

For intercity travel, Thailand has a robust **bus and train network.** Long-distance buses are comfortable and budget-friendly, with routes connecting Bangkok to Chiang Mai, Phuket, Krabi, and beyond. A VIP air-conditioned bus from Bangkok to Chiang Mai (an 8–10-hour journey) costs about **$20 to $30 USD.** The **railway system** is another scenic option, especially the overnight sleeper trains between Bangkok and northern destinations like Chiang Mai. A second-class sleeper ticket can cost around **$25 to $35 USD**, depending on the class and route.

For island hopping, **ferries and speedboats** connect mainland hubs like Phuket, Krabi, and Surat Thani to islands such as Koh Phi Phi, Koh Samui, and Koh Tao. One-way ferry tickets typically range from **$10 to $20 USD**. On the islands, tourists often rent **motorbikes or scooters** to explore, with daily rental rates between **$5 to $10 USD**—though caution and an international driver's permit are recommended for safety and legal reasons.

Domestic flights are a convenient option for covering long distances quickly. Budget airlines like **Thai AirAsia, Nok Air**, and **Thai Lion Air** offer frequent, low-cost flights between cities such as Bangkok, Chiang Mai, Phuket, and Krabi. With advance booking, one-way fares often range from **$25 to $60 USD**, including taxes.

Monetary Advice

Thailand's national currency is the **Thai Baht** (THB). As of mid-2025, **1 USD is roughly equivalent to 36–37 THB**, though exchange rates may fluctuate, so it's wise to check rates before exchanging money. Currency exchange is easy and widely available—at airports, banks, hotels, and dedicated currency exchange booths. Exchange rates are usually better at city exchange counters (like SuperRich in Bangkok) than at airports. ATMs are everywhere and accept most international cards, but expect a **withdrawal fee of around 220 THB** (about $6 USD) per transaction.

Credit and debit cards (Visa and Mastercard) are accepted in mid- to high-end hotels, restaurants, and larger stores. However, cash is still preferred, especially in markets, street food stalls, small shops, and rural areas. It's a good idea to carry both card and cash for flexibility. While some tourist hotspots may accept USD or Euros in limited settings, **you'll almost always get a better deal by paying in baht.**

Bargaining is common in markets, street stalls, and with tuk-tuk drivers—though not in shopping malls or chain restaurants. It's expected, even encouraged, and should be done politely with a smile. As a rule of thumb, try offering **about 60–70% of the asking price** and work your way from there. If the seller seems firm, it's best to walk away or pay if you think it's fair.

Tipping is not mandatory in Thailand, but it is increasingly appreciated in tourist areas. In casual restaurants, rounding up the bill or leaving **10–20 THB (about $0.50 USD)** is a kind gesture. For hotel porters or housekeepers, **20–50 THB ($0.50–$1.50 USD)** is generous. At upscale restaurants, **a tip of 5–10%** is customary if service isn't already included in the bill. Tuk-tuk and taxi drivers don't expect tips, but rounding up to the nearest 10 or 20 baht is a nice touch.

Thai Hospitality

Thailand is famously known as **"The Land of Smiles,"** and this nickname is well earned. Thai people are widely recognized for their **warm, gentle, and respectful demeanor**, and hospitality is deeply embedded in their culture. Visitors often comment on the kindness of locals, their willingness to help strangers, and the sense of calm and courtesy in everyday interactions. Whether you're staying in a family-run guesthouse or a five-star resort, you'll likely be greeted with a genuine smile and a desire to make your experience comfortable and memorable.

Hospitality in Thailand is often expressed through **graciousness, generosity**, and **calm communication**. Guests are treated with care and respect and hosts often go out of their way to assist—even if language barriers exist. The traditional greeting, the **wai** (a slight bow with palms pressed together in a prayer-like gesture), is a common way to show friendliness and respect. As a visitor, returning the wai when someone greets you this way is considered very polite.

Thai culture places a high value on **respect, humility**, and **harmony**, so understanding local etiquette goes a long way. It's considered polite to speak softly, smile often, and avoid confrontation or loud behavior, especially in public places. Pointing your feet at people or religious objects, touching someone's head, or displaying anger are all seen as disrespectful. Modesty in dress, especially when visiting temples, is important—cover shoulders, knees, and avoid wearing revealing clothes. Always remove your shoes before entering someone's home or a temple, and never climb on or touch Buddha statues.

To show respect for Thai culture as a visitor, **learn a few basic Thai phrases**, like "**Sawasdee**" (hello) and "**Khob khun**" (thank you), and use them with a smile. Be mindful of Thai customs, ask before taking photos of people (especially monks), and support local businesses by shopping at markets or eating at family-run restaurants. Observing and honoring these social cues will not only enrich your travel experience but will also be deeply appreciated by the people you meet.

CUSTOMS

IN THIS CHAPTER

- Travelers Entering Thailand
- Customs Entitlements and Monetary Restrictions
- Restricted and Prohibited Items
- Five Practical Tips to Know Before You Go

CUSTOMS

Travelers Entering Thailand

To enter Thailand in 2025, travelers must hold a passport that is valid for at least six months from the date of entry and contains at least one blank page for the entry stamp. Many nationalities, including citizens of the US, UK, EU, and several Asian countries, can enter Thailand without a visa for up to 60 days under the visa exemption program. This stay may be extended once by 30 days through immigration offices inside Thailand. Those entering via land or sea may face different rules depending on their nationality.

A key new requirement is the **Thailand Digital Arrival Card** (**TDAC**), which replaced the paper TM6 form in May 2025. All travelers (except airside transit passengers) must complete the TDAC online within 72 hours **prior** to arrival. The form asks for basic personal information, passport details, travel plans, accommodation in Thailand, and health/financial declarations. Once submitted, travelers receive a digital confirmation (PDF) that must be presented at immigration. There is no fee for the TDAC, and travelers should only use the official Thai Immigration Bureau website to avoid scam websites.

In addition, Thailand is gradually introducing an **Electronic Travel Authorization** (**ETA**) **system.** By mid-2025, most visa-exempt travelers will be required to obtain ETA approval prior to travel. This process is online, generates a QR code, and facilitates access to automated immigration gates at major Thai airports. Yellow fever vaccination certificates are required only if travelers are coming from designated endemic countries. Immigration officers may also ask for proof of onward or return travel and proof of sufficient funds for the stay.

Upon arrival in Thailand, travelers go through standard immigration and customs checks. If eligible and pre-registered through ETA, they may be allowed to use automated passport gates. While there are no COVID-related health screenings currently in place, travelers from high-risk countries may still undergo basic health checks. In terms of security, travelers should expect a normal but alert security presence, particularly at large airports and transport hubs.

Travelers should also be aware of a **few important advisories**. Thailand remains generally safe, but protests and demonstrations, particularly in Bangkok or near government buildings, can occur. It is recommended to avoid those areas. Travelers should be especially cautious in the far southern provinces of Yala, Narathiwat, and Pattani due to long-standing insurgent activity. Road safety is another concern, with motorbike accidents being common, particularly among tourists. It's advised to wear helmets, avoid night riding, and carry a valid license if renting scooters. Petty scams, drink-spiking, and police extortion (asking for "tea money") are occasionally reported in tourist hotspots.

Bear in mind that Thailand has **strict laws, particularly around defaming the monarchy (lese-majesté), drug possession, and behavior deemed disrespectful.** For official travel advisories, the U.S. State Department currently ranks Thailand at **Level 1: Exercise Normal Precautions**, with increased caution advised in the southern provinces, but you should always consult the safety advisory before traveling in case circumstances change.

Customs Entitlements and Monetary Restrictions

When traveling to Thailand, it's essential to be aware of the customs and monetary rules that apply upon arrival and departure. If you are entering or leaving with foreign currency **over $20,000 USD (or its equivalent),** a declaration is mandatory. Failure to declare such amounts may be treated as a **criminal offense**. For Thai baht, you may bring in unlimited amounts; however, when departing, carrying more than **50,000 THB per person (or 100,000 THB per family)** must be declared, and for travel to neighboring countries, the limit is up to 500,000 THB.

As for goods, Thailand allows a personal exemption: items for personal use worth up to **80,000 THB ($2,150 USD) per person** or **40,000 THB ($1,075 USD) per family** can generally be imported duty-free, provided they are reasonable in quantity and not restricted or prohibited. Additionally, specific limits apply to alcohol and tobacco—up to **1 L of spirits or wine** and either **200 cigarettes or 250 g of tobacco products per person**. Items exceeding these allowances or intended for commercial use must be declared and may incur duties or taxes.[1]

Thailand uses a **green/red corridor system**: travelers without dutiable goods proceed via the green channel, while those with declared or restricted items use the red channel.

Regarding food and health products, travelers may bring limited quantities for personal use. Up to **10 kg (22 lbs)** of meat or processed animal products and **2.5–5 kg (5–11 lbs)** of dairy, snacks, coffee, herbs, and similar goods are generally permitted. Cosmetics are limited to three units per type with a maximum of **15 items in total**. Prescription medicines and certain herbal or psychotropic products require proper documentation—such as a medical certificate, doctor's prescription, or official permits—depending on the substance and the supply length.

 ## Restricted and Prohibited Items

When preparing for a trip to Thailand, it's important to understand the country's customs regulations regarding what items are allowed,

---

1   https://www.customs.go.th/

restricted, or completely prohibited at the border. Thai authorities enforce these rules strictly to protect public safety, cultural heritage, and the environment. Travelers carrying banned or controlled items—whether knowingly or not—may face serious legal consequences, including fines, confiscation, or even imprisonment. To ensure a smooth and lawful entry, it's essential to know in advance what you can and cannot bring into Thailand, and to follow the correct procedures for any restricted goods.

Restricted items, which require permission or documentation to import, include:

- Firearms, ammunition, explosives, and weapons (permit required from Thai authorities)
- Prescription medications, especially those containing psychotropic substances (documentation and sometimes permits required)
- Controlled or non-FDA-approved medicines and health supplements
- Buddha images, religious artifacts, or antiques (require export or import permits from the Fine Arts Department)
- Live animals, animal products, and plants (permits required from the Department of Livestock Development or Agriculture)
- Drones and telecommunications equipment (must be registered with Thai regulators)
- Large lithium batteries or power banks exceeding airline safety thresholds
- Certain cosmetics, herbal remedies, and food supplements (subject to quantity restrictions or health registration)
- Cultural items or historical artifacts (require verification and clearance)

Prohibited items, strictly forbidden to bring into Thailand, include:

- Narcotics and illegal drugs (e.g., heroin, cocaine, methamphetamine, cannabis)
- Pornographic materials or obscene publications

- Counterfeit goods, including fake brand-name products and pirated media

- Fake currency or documents with forged official seals

- Electronic cigarettes, vaping devices, e-liquids, and shisha

- Items infringing on intellectual property (e.g., unauthorized software or media)

- Wildlife products and parts from endangered species (e.g., ivory, rhino horn)

- Obscene images or materials deemed offensive to Thai culture or public morality

Five Practical Tips to Know Before You Go

1. **Dress Modestly at Temples and Sacred Sites:** Thailand is a deeply Buddhist country, and proper attire is essential when visiting temples. Always cover your shoulders and knees, and remove your shoes before entering temple buildings. Wearing respectful clothing shows appreciation for Thai customs and avoids offending locals or being denied entry.

2. **Respect the Royal Family:** Any form of disrespect toward the Thai monarchy is a serious offense under lese-majesté laws. Avoid making jokes or comments about the royal family, and always stand still during the national anthem (played in cinemas and at public events). Thais show deep reverence, and visitors are expected to do the same.

3. **Use the Wai Gesture Appropriately:** The traditional Thai greeting, called a wai, involves placing your palms together at chest level and bowing slightly. It's a sign of respect, especially when greeting elders, monks, or in formal settings. Return a wai when offered, but don't initiate it with service workers or children, as it's not expected.

4. **Take Off Your Shoes Indoors:** In Thai culture, the feet are considered the lowest and dirtiest part of the body. Always remove

your shoes when entering someone's home, small shops, and even some offices or restaurants. Look for shoe racks at the entrance as a cue.

5. **Carry Small Change for Street Vendors and Transport:** Cash is king in many parts of Thailand, especially in markets, taxis, and rural areas. While larger businesses may accept cards, it's wise to carry small denominations of Thai baht for smooth transactions. A polite smile and a few Thai words like "khop khun ka/krap" (thank you) go a long way in making everyday interactions more pleasant.

CRIME IN THAILAND

CRIME IN THAILAND

Overview

Thailand is generally considered a **safe country for travelers and residents** alike. Violent crime is relatively rare in most parts of the country, particularly in areas frequented by tourists such as Bangkok, Chiang Mai, Phuket, and the islands. However, like many tourist destinations, there are risks of petty crimes such as pickpocketing, bag-snatching, and scams—especially in busy markets, nightlife areas, and transport hubs. These incidents are usually non-violent and opportunistic in nature.

Several factors contribute to crime in Thailand. The high volume of tourism can attract **scammers and petty criminals** who target foreigners. **Road safety** is another area of concern—Thailand consistently ranks among the countries with the highest traffic fatality rates in the world, particularly involving motorcycles. **Drug-related crime remains a challenge**, with increased activity linked to trafficking routes from neighboring countries. **Corruption**, particularly at lower administrative levels, and a lack of consistent enforcement can also contribute to certain types of local crime. In the southern border provinces of Yala, Pattani, and Narathiwat, **separatist violence** remains a serious issue, although it is largely isolated from the rest of the country.

Crime trends over time in Thailand show that the overall crime rate has declined significantly over the past two decades. **Violent crime**, including homicide, has remained **relatively stable and low**. However, recent years have seen a notable rise in cybercrime and financial fraud, including online scams and investment fraud schemes. Additionally, drug trafficking activity has surged, driven by instability in neighboring countries and increased methamphetamine production in the region. Despite these issues, most visitors experience Thailand as a welcoming and secure destination, provided they take normal precautions.

Crime Hotspots in Thailand

Thailand is generally regarded as a **safe destination for tourists**, though certain areas have higher crime rates that travelers should be aware of. Major cities like **Bangkok**, particularly busy markets and nightlife districts such as **Khao San Road** and **Patpong**, as well as popular tourist hubs like **Pattaya** and **Phuket**, tend to experience more **petty crimes** like **pickpocketing, bag-snatching**, and various **tourist scams**. While violent crime against visitors in these areas is uncommon, petty crime remains a frequent nuisance. More serious security concerns exist in the southern border provinces of **Yala, Pattani**, and **Narathiwat**, where an ongoing **insurgency** has led to violence including **bombings** and **armed attacks**. These provinces are generally considered **unsafe for travel** and are frequently flagged in **international travel advisories**.

Comparatively, Thailand's overall **violent crime rate is lower than that of the United States**. For example, Thailand's homicide rate is approximately 2.4 per 100,000 people, which is below the U.S. rate that averages around 5 per 100,000, though regional differences exist in both countries. However, Thailand faces significant challenges with **road safety**, with **traffic fatalities** far exceeding those in the U.S., largely due to high rates of **motorcycle accidents** and less stringent enforcement of **traffic laws**.

Law enforcement effectiveness in Thailand is **mixed**. While many officers perform professionally, **corruption** and **bribery** remain notable problems at local levels, sometimes leading to **inconsistent enforcement** of laws. This corruption can undermine trust and allow petty crimes to flourish with little consequence. Tourists occasionally face demands for **informal payments**, which can complicate interactions with authorities and affect perceptions of safety.

Despite these challenges, violent crimes against tourists remain relatively rare. The most common issues travelers face are **petty theft**, **scams** involving **overcharging** or **fake services**, **rigged taxi fares**, and occasional **credit card fraud** or **online scams** targeting foreigners. By exercising vigilance, using reputable services, and securing belongings, visitors generally experience Thailand as a safe and welcoming destination.

For up-to-date travel warnings and advice, official sources like the **U.S. Department of State's travel advisory** offer valuable guidance on safety, security risks, and areas to avoid.

Quick Safety Tips

- Always keep your valuables secure and avoid carrying large amounts of cash or flashy jewelry, especially in crowded areas and markets.

- Use licensed taxis or ride-hailing apps like Grab to avoid scams or overcharging; agree on fares beforehand if using traditional taxis.

- Stay vigilant when visiting busy tourist spots and avoid distractions that could make you a target for pickpockets or bag-snatchers.

- Be cautious when accepting offers for tours or services from street vendors; book through reputable agencies or your hotel to avoid scams.

- When traveling by motorcycle or scooter, always wear a helmet and drive defensively, as road accidents are a leading cause of injury.

- Avoid traveling to the southern border provinces of Yala, Pattani, and Narathiwat, where ongoing security concerns make these areas unsafe for tourists.

CRIMINAL LAW VIOLATIONS

CHAPTER 4

CRIMINAL LAW VIOLATIONS

Marijuana and Other Drugs in Thailand

Thailand has a **long and complex history with cannabis** and other drugs. Traditionally, cannabis was used in Thai herbal medicine and local culture for centuries, valued for its medicinal and therapeutic properties. However, starting in the mid-20th century, Thailand adopted strict narcotics laws influenced by international drug control policies, classifying cannabis and other substances as illegal. The government implemented harsh penalties for possession, trafficking, and use, reflecting a zero-tolerance approach that persisted for decades.

This stance began to shift in recent years. In **2018**, Thailand made headlines as **the first Southeast Asian country to legalize medical marijuana**, signaling a significant change in drug policy. **Medical cannabis** is now **legally prescribed** for patients suffering from chronic pain, epilepsy, multiple sclerosis, and other qualifying conditions. The government established a regulatory framework that allows licensed hospitals and clinics to produce and dispense cannabis-based medicines. Public institutions and private enterprises have also been encouraged to participate in medical cannabis research and development, making Thailand a regional pioneer in this space.[2]

---

2   https://time.com/7298262/thailand-cannabis-marijuana-weed-recriminalization-delegalization-pheu-thai-new-policy/

Nevertheless, despite these advances, **recreational marijuana remains illegal**. Possession, use, or sale of cannabis for recreational purposes can result in severe penalties, including **fines and imprisonment**. Public smoking of marijuana is discouraged and can attract fines, even for patients legally using medical cannabis. The government emphasizes that medical legalization does not equate to recreational legalization, maintaining strict controls to prevent abuse.

In addition to natural cannabis, Thailand has faced challenges with **synthetic cannabinoids**—chemically produced substances designed to mimic THC's effects. Often marketed as "herbal incense" or "spice," these drugs can be much more potent and unpredictable, leading to serious health risks and sometimes fatal overdoses. Thai authorities **actively ban synthetic cannabinoids** and conduct regular crackdowns to control their distribution.

The legal framework surrounding marijuana in Thailand includes specific rules and limitations. Patients must receive a prescription from a licensed medical professional and are only allowed to possess limited amounts of cannabis products. Commercial cultivation and sales are tightly regulated, and unlicensed activities remain criminal offenses. Additionally, smoking cannabis in public places is prohibited, aligning with public health policies.

Beyond cannabis, Thailand maintains **strict drug laws covering a wide range of controlled substances**. These include methamphetamine ("yaba"), heroin, cocaine, opium, and synthetic drugs. Thailand's strategic location along major drug trafficking routes in Southeast Asia has made it a hotspot for drug production and smuggling. Consequently, the government enforces **harsh penalties** for drug offenses, including **long prison sentences and even the death penalty for serious trafficking crimes**. The authorities also run extensive anti-drug campaigns and collaborate with international agencies to combat drug trafficking.

Visitors and residents alike should exercise caution and fully comply with Thailand's drug laws. Despite recent medical marijuana reforms, **drug possession and use outside approved medical contexts remain illegal and can lead to severe consequences,** including arrest, prosecution, and imprisonment. Being informed and respectful of local regulations is essential for anyone traveling to or living in Thailand.

Prescription Medication

When traveling to Thailand with prescription or over-the-counter (OTC) medications, it is important to follow the country's strict regulations to avoid legal issues. Travelers may bring prescription medications **for personal use**, but generally only **up to a 30-day supply** is allowed without needing special permission. It is essential to carry the original prescription or a doctor's letter that includes the patient's name, medical condition, medication details, dosage, and the prescribing physician's information. For medications containing narcotic or psychotropic substances, **prior approval from the Thai Food and Drug Administration (FDA) is required**, and applications should be submitted at least 15 days before travel.

Regarding over-the-counter medications, some common medicines available elsewhere may be restricted in Thailand. For example, medications containing pseudoephedrine, certain antibiotics, or other controlled substances could be classified as restricted. It is advisable to verify whether any OTC medication is restricted or controlled by consulting with the Thai FDA before traveling.

Violating Thailand's medication importation regulations can lead to serious consequences. Travelers caught with unauthorized medications may face **substantial fines**, and in severe cases, they could be **detained and deported**, especially if carrying large quantities of controlled substances. **Criminal prosecution** is also a possibility for violations involving controlled substances, which may result in imprisonment, heavy fines, and a permanent ban from entering Thailand.

To avoid complications, travelers should research Thailand's customs regulations and controlled substances list prior to their trip. Discussing medications with a healthcare provider ensures that all necessary documentation is in order. Additionally, contacting the Thai embassy or consulate in the traveler's home country can provide guidance on specific medications. For those bringing prescription or controlled medications, consulting a legal professional in Thailand before traveling is recommended to ensure compliance with local laws. By taking these precautions, travelers can have a smooth and hassle-free experience during their stay in Thailand.

Penalties

In Thailand, penalties for marijuana and other drug offenses are **among the strictest in the world,** reflecting the government's tough stance on narcotics. Despite recent reforms legalizing medical marijuana, possession, use, sale, or trafficking of marijuana outside medical guidelines remains illegal and subject to severe punishment.

For marijuana-related offenses, penalties vary depending on the amount and intent:

- Possession of **small amounts for personal use** (without medical authorization) can lead to **fines, imprisonment, or both.**
- Possession of **larger quantities or intent to sell/traffic** results in much harsher penalties, including long prison terms. Trafficking large amounts of marijuana can carry sentences of 10 to 15 years or more.
- **Cultivation of cannabis** without a license is also illegal and punishable by imprisonment and fines.
- **Public smoking or consumption** outside authorized medical settings may result in **fines or detention.**

For hard drugs, Thailand enforces extremely strict laws:

- Possession of even **small amounts of hard drugs** may result in imprisonment ranging from **several years to life sentences.**
- **Trafficking or distribution** of large quantities of these drugs can result in life **imprisonment or the death penalty.** Thailand is known for capital punishment in drug trafficking cases, making it one of the countries with the toughest penalties in Asia.

Thai law allows for mandatory rehabilitation programs for some drug users, especially those caught with smaller quantities and no intent to traffic, but this is at the discretion of authorities. Given these severe penalties, travelers and residents should strictly avoid any involvement with illegal drugs. Even medical marijuana users should ensure they follow all legal requirements closely to avoid prosecution.

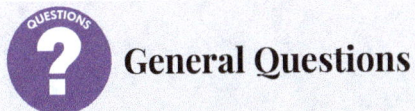

General Questions

1. *Is cannabis legal in Thailand?* Partially. Cannabis is **legal** in Thailand **only for medical use** with a valid prescription from a licensed healthcare professional. Recreational use, public consumption, and unauthorized sale remain illegal and can result in fines and imprisonment.

2. *Where can I legally purchase marijuana in Thailand?* You can legally purchase marijuana in Thailand only at **licensed medical dispensaries** or **government hospitals and clinics** with a valid prescription from a licensed healthcare professional. Recreational sales and purchases are illegal.

3. *Can I have marijuana on my person or in hotel room in Thailand?* You can only have marijuana on your person or in your hotel room in Thailand **only if you have a valid medical prescription**. Possessing cannabis without authorization is illegal and can lead to fines or imprisonment.

4. *Are there any other exceptions to the possession and consumption of cannabis in Thailand?* The only exception for possession and consumption of cannabis in Thailand is for **medical use with a valid prescription** from a licensed healthcare professional. Public smoking and recreational use remain illegal.

5. *What are the penalties for possessing and consuming other types of illicit drugs in Thailand?* Penalties for possessing or consuming illicit drugs in Thailand are very **severe**. Possession of hard drugs like methamphetamine or heroin can lead to up to 10 years in prison and heavy fines. Trafficking these drugs may result in life imprisonment or the death penalty. Lesser drugs still carry prison terms and fines, and recent laws may offer rehabilitation for small personal-use amounts.

 ## Law of the Land Hypothetical

HYPOTHETICAL: *James is traveling to Thailand for a two-week vacation. He needs to bring his prescription medication for anxiety, which contains a controlled substance. He has the medication in its original packaging but does not have a doctor's letter or prior approval from Thai authorities. At customs, officials ask for documentation, and James is unsure what to do.*

Can James legally bring his prescription anxiety medication containing a controlled substance into Thailand without prior approval or a doctor's letter?

ANSWER: *No. James **cannot** legally bring his prescription medication containing a controlled substance into Thailand without prior approval from the Thai Food and Drug Administration and proper documentation such as a doctor's letter or prescription. Thailand requires travelers carrying narcotic or psychotropic medications to obtain permission before arrival. Without this, James risks having his medication confiscated, facing fines, detention, or even criminal charges. To avoid such issues, travelers should obtain the necessary approvals and carry appropriate documentation before entering Thailand.*

Takeaways

- Thailand has a complex history with cannabis and drugs, moving from traditional medicinal use to strict narcotics laws influenced by international policy. While medical marijuana has been legalized under tight regulations, **recreational use remains illegal** and heavily penalized.

- Travelers bringing prescription or over-the-counter medications must comply with Thailand's strict import rules, including **carrying original prescriptions and obtaining prior approval for controlled substances**. Failure to do so can result in fines, detention, or deportation.

- Penalties for drug offenses in Thailand are **among the harshest globally**. Possession, trafficking, or cultivation of marijuana without authorization can lead to long prison sentences and heavy fines. Hard drugs carry even more severe punishments, including the death penalty for trafficking large amounts.

- Medical marijuana use is permitted **only with a valid prescription from licensed professionals** and must be obtained through authorized dispensaries. Possession or consumption outside medical guidelines, including public smoking or recreational use, remains illegal and punishable.

- Travelers should **always verify medication regulations and drug laws before arriving in Thailand**, ensuring all necessary documentation is in order. Ignorance of these laws offers no protection, and violations can result in serious legal consequences.

ALCOHOL-RELATED OFFENSES

ALCOHOL-RELATED OFFENSES

Alcohol-Related Offenses

Alcohol in Thailand holds a nuanced place in society, blending long-standing cultural practices with modern-day regulations and commercial interests. While traditional Thai society—strongly influenced by **Buddhist teachings**—historically encouraged temperance or abstinence from alcohol, especially among monks and the devout, drinking has become a common feature of social interaction, particularly in urban and tourist-heavy areas. Alcohol is typically enjoyed during weddings, New Year festivals like **Songkran**, village celebrations, and casual gatherings among friends. However, in rural or deeply religious areas, alcohol consumption is less prominent and often carries a stigma.

Thailand's alcohol market is robust and includes both **locally-produced beverages** and a wide range of imported products. Thai beers such as **Singha, Chang**, and **Leo** are national staples, while spirits like **Mekhong** (sometimes called "Thai whiskey," though technically a rum) and **SangSom** are popular among locals and tourists alike. In more upscale bars or resorts, international wines and cocktails made with tropical ingredients are widely available.

Although **alcohol is legal and accessible**, it is subject to **strict laws** governing its sale and consumption as well as **tight restrictions on alcohol advertising**. Violating these rules can result in hefty fines for businesses and individuals. This reflects the government's ongoing public health campaign to reduce alcohol abuse, which remains a concern in some demographics.

Overall, while alcohol is a significant part of Thailand's modern lifestyle and tourism industry, visitors should be aware of **legal boundaries, cultural sensitivities**, and the consequences of misuse. Respecting these norms ensures a safer and more culturally informed travel experience.

Alcohol Regulation

Thailand enforces a comprehensive set of regulations around the sale, consumption, and advertisement of alcohol, reflecting a balance between its thriving tourism industry, public health concerns, and cultural values. While alcohol is legal and widely consumed, particularly in social settings and tourist areas, there are clear restrictions designed to control its availability and limit its societal impact.

The **legal drinking age** in Thailand is **20**, and it is illegal to sell alcohol to anyone under this age. Vendors are required to check identification, and failure to comply can result in heavy fines or even imprisonment. Alcohol sales are also **limited to specific hours**: permitted only between **11:00 a.m. and 2:00 p.m.**, and again from 5:00 p.m. to midnight. Outside these hours, sales are banned, even in supermarkets and convenience stores.[3]

Alcohol sales are **prohibited on certain religious and national holidays**, particularly important **Buddhist holy days** such as Makha Bucha, Visakha Bucha, and Asalha Bucha. On election days, alcohol sales are also forbidden from the evening before through the end of the election day, to discourage voter influence and disorderly behavior.

In terms of location, alcohol cannot be sold near **educational institutions, government buildings, or temples,** and some public areas such as parks, sports stadiums, and public transport hubs may be designated

---

3   https://www.nationthailand.com/news/policy/40051813

alcohol-free zones. These regulations are actively enforced, especially in more conservative provinces or during national events.

Thailand also maintains **strict advertising laws** regarding alcohol. Advertisements cannot depict people drinking or suggest that alcohol enhances attractiveness, success, or social status. Even online content is regulated, and influencers or businesses caught violating these laws may face fines of up to **500,000 THB** (about $13,500 USD) or imprisonment. Likewise, drinking and driving laws are also strict. The legal blood alcohol limit is **0.05%** for most drivers and **0.02%** for professional or new drivers. Police conduct routine sobriety checkpoints, especially in urban nightlife areas, and violators face stiff penalties including **license suspension, fines, mandatory education, or jail time.**[4]

Overall, Thailand's alcohol regulation reflects a dual reality: while alcohol is accessible and socially accepted in many settings, it is surrounded by firm legal boundaries intended to promote public safety, uphold religious respect, and mitigate abuse. Visitors are advised to respect these laws to avoid serious consequences.

 **Things to Remember**

- **Drinking Age:** The legal drinking age in Thailand is **20 years old.** It is illegal to sell or serve alcohol to anyone under this age, and violators—both sellers and underage drinkers—can face fines and imprisonment.

- **ID:** You must present **valid photo identification** (e.g., passport or Thai national ID card) to purchase alcohol, especially in convenience stores, supermarkets, and bars. Vendors are legally required to verify the buyer's age.

---

4   https://www.unescap.org/sites/default/files/Country%20statement%20
-%20Thailand-%20Relevant%20Laws%20related%20to%20Drink%20
Driving.pdf

- **Public Consumption:** Drinking alcohol **in public spaces** like streets, parks, religious sites, government offices, and public transport stations is **prohibited**. Violations may result in fines and, in some cases, confiscation of alcohol.

- **Public Drunkenness:** While mild public intoxication may be tolerated in nightlife areas, **disruptive behavior** due to intoxication can lead to **arrest, fines, or even jail time**, particularly if it disturbs others or violates local decorum.

- **Drunk Driving:** The legal blood alcohol concentration (BAC) limit is **0.05% for regular drivers** and **0.02% for new or professional drivers**. Penalties include **fines, imprisonment, license suspension, and mandatory rehab or education programs**. Refusal to take a breath test is also punishable.

- **Purchase of Alcohol:** Alcohol can legally be purchased only between **11:00 a.m. – 2:00 p.m.** and **5:00 p.m. – midnight**, with exceptions for bars, clubs, and international airport terminals. Sales are **banned on major Buddhist holidays and election days**. It is illegal to sell alcohol near schools, temples, and government offices.

- **Alcohol Permits:** A special **alcohol sales permit is required** for selling alcohol at private events, parties, or festivals, especially if the event is commercial or open to the public. For private house parties with no alcohol sales, a permit is generally not needed unless loud noise or large crowds attract police attention.

- **Illegal Alcohol:** Unregulated or **illegally produced alcohol** (often referred to as "moonshine" or home-brew) is a public health issue in some rural areas. It can contain dangerous levels of methanol. Possession, sale, or distribution of such alcohol is **illegal** and can result in **severe penalties**, including **imprisonment and fines**.

General Questions

1. *Can I drink and drive in Thailand?* **No**. Drinking and driving is **illegal** in Thailand. The legal blood alcohol limit is **0.05%**, and for drivers under 20 or with provisional licenses, it's **0.02%**. Violations can result in fines, imprisonment, license suspension, and mandatory rehabilitation.

2. *Can I possess an open container in public?* **No**. Possessing or consuming alcohol in public places in Thailand—such as streets, parks, public transport, temples, and government buildings—is generally **prohibited**. While enforcement may be more relaxed in some tourist areas, the law allows police to issue **fines or detain individuals** for drinking in public. It's safest to consume alcohol only in private settings or licensed venues to avoid legal issues.

Law of the Land Hypothetical

HYPOTHETICAL: *David, a tourist visiting Bangkok, buys a bottle of local whiskey from a convenience store at 3:00 p.m. and on the way home, a police officer stops him and asks for the receipt. Did David do something illegal?*

ANSWER: *Yes. In Thailand, alcohol sales are only permitted between 11:00 a.m. and 2:00 p.m., and then again from 5:00 p.m. to midnight. Purchasing alcohol at 3:00 p.m. is outside the allowed sale hours and is therefore illegal. If caught, David could face fines, and the vendor might also be penalized. Tourists should be aware of these restrictions to avoid legal trouble.*

Takeaways

- Alcohol is legal but **tightly regulated** in Thailand. While widely consumed and available—especially in urban and tourist areas—the government enforces strict rules on when, where, and how alcohol can be purchased and consumed.

- The **legal drinking age is 20**, and both sellers and underage consumers can face fines or imprisonment for violations. ID checks are required, and vendors are obligated to comply with the law.

- **Public consumption** is **restricted**. Drinking alcohol in public places such as streets, parks, and near temples or government buildings is generally prohibited and can result in fines or detention.

- Drunk driving is harshly punished. Thailand enforces strict blood alcohol limits (**0.05%** for regular drivers, **0.02%** for new/professional drivers). Penalties include jail time, fines, license suspension, and mandatory rehab.

- Alcohol sales are **restricted** by time and occasion. Legal sales occur only between **11 a.m. – 2 p.m.** and **5 p.m. – midnight**. Sales are banned on major religious holidays and election days. Special permits are needed for alcohol at events, and illegal or unregulated alcohol remains a public health and legal concern.

FIREARM & AMMUNITION OFFENSES

CHAPTER 6

FIREARM & AMMUNITION OFFENSES

Current Firearm Status and Related Penalties[5]

Thailand's current firearm situation is shaped by strict legal regulations, a high rate of gun ownership, and recent efforts to tighten control in response to growing concerns about public safety. Firearms are governed primarily by the **1947 Firearms Act, amended in 2017,** alongside other laws like the **Arms Control Act** and the **Thai Penal Code**. Thailand is estimated to have over 10 million firearms in circulation, with around 6.2 million registered.[6] The rest are believed to be unregistered or illegal, including homemade weapons, smuggled firearms, or converted blank guns. Civilian gun ownership is the highest in Southeast Asia, at roughly 15 guns per 100 people. A longstanding welfare program allows police and military personnel to buy guns at reduced prices, further boosting numbers. Despite strict licensing, illegal firearms remain widely available on the black market and are implicated in most gun-related crimes and mass shootings.

In response to rising gun violence, particularly following several high-profile mass shootings since 2020, the Thai government imposed a one-year suspension starting late 2023 on issuing new carry permits

---

5   https://www.siam-legal.com/thailand-law/are-guns-legal-in-thailand

6   https://en.wikipedia.org/wiki/Firearms_in_Thailand

and halted new import licenses for firearms, blank guns, and replicas. Customs checks and firearm documentation have also been tightened. A new draft bill passed in early 2024 mandates the registration of all guns and ammunition within 180 days of enactment. Upcoming reforms will also include medical and psychological assessments for applicants, stricter controls over gun stores, and attempts to close regulatory loopholes.

Despite these efforts, enforcement challenges persist. Much of the public perceives current laws as strong on paper but poorly enforced, with illegal guns continuing to circulate widely. Social attitudes in Thailand treat gun ownership as a symbol of protection and status, and many believe that the core issue lies in enforcement rather than the laws themselves. These factors complicate government attempts to control the firearm landscape. While legislative momentum is growing, especially in the wake of recent tragedies, a lasting reduction in gun violence will likely require more than legal reform—it will demand improved enforcement, better monitoring of existing weapons, and a cultural shift in how firearms are viewed in Thai society.

According to Thai law, **only Thai citizens are allowed to own or possess firearms.** Applicants for firearm licenses must be **at least 20 years** old, have a **clean criminal record**, be **mentally and physically fit**, and demonstrate a **stable income** and **permanent residence** in Thailand. Additionally, applicants must have their name registered on a Thai house registration document (Tabien Baan) for a minimum of six months in the province where they apply. Licensing falls under the jurisdiction of the local district or provincial administration.

There are **multiple firearm license types. A Por.1 license** is needed to **purchase a firearm**. After purchase, the gun must be registered under a **Por.4 license** to **possess and store it**. To carry a firearm in public, which is strictly controlled, a separate **Por.12 (concealed carry) license** must be obtained. This is rarely granted and only under special conditions, such as documented personal threats or professional necessity. License fees **vary based on the firearm**. The application involves form submission, background checks, in some cases interviews, and approvals from local authorities. Once licensed, firearms must be stored securely at the registered location, and any use outside that location without additional permits is prohibited.

Carrying a firearm in public without a Por.12, even if legally owned and registered, is **illegal**. Violations can lead to imprisonment of **1–10 years** and fines ranging from **2,000 THB to 20,000 THB (approximately $55–$550 USD)**. The laws surrounding firearms are strict and rigorously enforced. Unauthorized possession of a firearm is considered a serious criminal offense; even simply carrying a firearm in public without a valid reason is criminalized, regardless of whether the firearm is licensed. Individuals who violate this law may be sentenced to **up to 5 years** in prison and fined up to **10,000 THB (approximately $275 USD)**. The penalties become more severe if a firearm is discharged in a public place. Firing a gun in public—regardless of whether it causes injury—is punishable by a prison sentence ranging from **6 months to 5 years**, and often accompanied by a fine. If the discharge results in injury, property damage, or death, the penalties increase dramatically. When a firearm is used intentionally to harm or kill, the offender may face **life imprisonment** or, in extreme cases, the **death penalty**. Engaging in the illegal sale, distribution, or smuggling of firearms is treated as an especially grave offense. Those convicted can be sentenced to between **10 and 20 years** in prison. Depending on the scale of the operation and the threat to public safety or national security, the penalties may be even more severe.

The 2017 legal amendments introduced stricter controls in response to rising gun violence and illegal firearms. Since then, enforcement has been stepped up. In late 2023, the Thai government imposed a one-year suspension on new applications for carry permits and firearm imports, including blank-firing guns and replicas. These restrictions followed high-profile shootings and were intended to close regulatory loopholes. Authorities have also cracked down on the modification of blank guns into lethal weapons.

Firearm Restrictions for Visitors

Non-citizens and visitors in Thailand are strictly prohibited from own-ing, purchasing, carrying, or using firearms. Thai firearm laws explicitly reserve gun ownership rights for Thai nationals only. This restriction in-cludes **permanent residents, long-term visa holders, foreign workers, and tourists.** The 2017 amendment to the Firearms Act reaffirmed and tightened these rules, barring all non-citizens from registering firearms under any circumstance, regardless of how long they have lived in the country or their legal status.

Foreigners are also not allowed to apply for a firearm license or per-mit, even for sport shooting or hunting purposes. Any foreign national found in possession of a firearm—whether legally registered to some-one else or unregistered—can face **severe criminal penalties, includ-ing imprisonment and deportation.** Visitors are not allowed to bring firearms into Thailand, even for temporary use or with permits from other countries. Attempting to import, transport, or declare a firearm at customs as a visitor will result in confiscation, legal action, and likely blacklisting. The only exceptions occur under very narrow circumstanc-es for diplomatic or official foreign security personnel, and these require **pre-authorization through government-to-government agreements** and specific Ministry of Interior approval. Even then, the firearms must be declared, approved before entry, and remain under strict control for the duration of use.

In summary, there are **no firearm rights granted to non-citizens or visitors** in Thailand. Any firearm activity is legally limited to Thai na-tionals with proper registration and licensing. Violation of these laws by foreigners results in serious consequences.

General Questions

1. *What happens if the police catch me carrying a firearm in Thailand?* If the police catch you carrying a firearm in Thailand, even without bullets, you will likely be arrested and face serious legal consequences. Thai law treats the act of carrying a firearm in public as a **criminal offense**, regardless of whether the weapon is loaded. The law does not require ammunition to be present for a charge to apply, because the firearm itself is considered a potential threat. If you do not have a proper carry permit—which is separate from a license to own the gun—you can be charged with illegal possession or illegal carrying of a weapon. If the gun is also unlicensed, the penalties increase significantly, potentially leading to ten years in prison and higher fines. For foreigners, the situation is even more severe, as being caught with a firearm can also lead to **deportation** and **being blacklisted from re-entering** the country. The Thai authorities enforce these laws strictly, and the fact that a gun is unloaded does not reduce the seriousness of the offense.

2. *What is the potential sentence for a firearms violation upon conviction?* In Thailand, if you're convicted of a firearms violation you can face serious penalties. Carrying a firearm in public without a carry permit can result in up to 5 years in prison and a fine of up to 10,000 THB (about $275 USD). If the firearm is unlicensed, the penalty increases to 1 to 10 years in prison and a fine of 2,000 to 20,000 THB (about $55–$550 USD). Foreigners face the same criminal penalties but may also be deported and banned from re-entering the country. While these fines may not seem high by Western standards, **they are considered substantial in Thailand**, where the average monthly income is significantly lower.

Law of the Land True Story[7]

In October 2023, a tragic shooting took place at Bangkok's Siam Paragon mall when a 14-year-old boy fired a modified blank-firing pistol, killing three people and injuring several others. The weapon had been illegally converted to fire real bullets, underscoring significant weaknesses in firearm control and enforcement in Thailand. The incident shocked the nation, raising alarm about how easily dangerous firearms—especially modified or illegal ones—could end up in the hands of minors or criminals. Public outrage grew over the accessibility of such weapons and the potential threat they posed to public safety, particularly in crowded urban areas.

In response to this tragedy and the resulting fear, the Thai government took swift action by suspending the issuance of new firearm carrying permits starting February 2025. This measure was aimed at tightening control over who can legally carry firearms in public and preventing further gun-related violence. The suspension reflects the government's commitment to reevaluating and strengthening firearm laws and licensing processes. Authorities hope that by pausing the issuance of new permits, they can reduce the risk of similar violent incidents and better protect citizens from gun violence in the future.

Takeaways

- Thailand has strict gun laws under the 1947 Firearms Act (amended 2017. Despite this, illegal firearms are widespread and linked to most gun crimes. In late 2023, the government suspended new carry permits and firearm imports amid rising gun violence, with

---

7   https://www.aljazeera.com/news/2023/10/5/two-men-arrested-over-gun-sale-to-teen-suspected-for-bangkok-mall-shooting

new reforms planned including mandatory registration and stricter licensing.

- Only Thai citizens can legally own or carry firearms. Non-citizens—including residents and tourists—are banned from owning, carrying, or using guns. Foreigners caught with firearms face imprisonment, deportation, and blacklisting, except for approved diplomats with special permits.

- Carrying a firearm without a proper permit is a criminal offense, even if unloaded, punishable by up to 10 years in prison and significant fines. Foreigners also risk deportation and ban from returning.

- Illegal carrying of licensed guns can lead to up to 5 years imprisonment and fines up to 10,000 THB ($270 USD). These fines are significant in Thailand's economy.

- Despite strong laws, enforcement remains a major challenge due to widespread illegal guns and social attitudes that view firearms as symbols of protection or status. The government is working to improve monitoring and enforcement, but lasting change will require cultural shifts alongside legal reforms.

PROSTITUTION

CHAPTER 7

PROSTITUTION

Overview[8]

Although prostitution is officially **illegal** in Thailand, it remains a deeply embedded and **highly visible part of the country's economy** and social fabric. The law criminalizes activities such as solicitation, brothel ownership, pimping, and exploiting sex workers, especially minors. Penalties can include fines, imprisonment, and business closures. Despite this legal framework, enforcement is often uneven, and many sex-related establishments operate under the guise of legitimate businesses like massage parlors, bars, or nightclubs.

The Thai sex industry is vast and diverse, ranging from high-end escort services and entertainment venues in tourist areas to informal street-based work. Estimates of the number of sex workers vary widely, but the figure is believed to be in the hundreds of thousands. Economic inequality, lack of opportunity, and migration from rural areas or neighboring countries contribute to the industry's size. While some individuals voluntarily enter sex work as a means of financial survival, others—particularly women and girls—are vulnerable to trafficking, coercion, or abuse.

Cultural attitudes toward sex work in Thailand are complex. It is often treated with a mix of tolerance, stigma, and moral ambiguity. The industry has **strong links to the tourism sector**, and while it draws criticism

---

8   https://thailawonline.com/prostitution-laws-in-thailand

from human rights organizations, it also generates significant income for many. In recent years, public discussion has grown around the need for legal reform, with some advocating for the decriminalization or regulation of sex work to improve worker safety and reduce exploitation. However, opposition remains strong from conservative and religious factions, and real policy change has been slow.

Laws and Penalties

Prostitution in Thailand is **technically illegal** under the **Prevention and Suppression of Prostitution Act of 1996**, which criminalizes the selling of sex, public solicitation, operating brothels, profiting from prostitution, and engaging in commercial sex with minors. Despite this, the sex trade remains widespread and often operates openly, especially in well-known nightlife zones such as **Patpong**, **Nana Plaza**, and **Soi Cowboy** in Bangkok, **Walking Street** in Pattaya, and **Bangla Road** in Phuket. Although these areas are not officially designated red-light districts, they function as such due to a longstanding culture of tolerance and informal arrangements with local officials.

Regulation in these zones is mostly informal, with some venues facing **occasional inspections** or making unofficial payments to avoid interference. Enforcement is **inconsistent** and often reactive, typically prompted by international pressure or high-profile trafficking cases. Because prostitution is not recognized as legal work, there are **no formal labor protections or licensing requirements** for sex workers. While some venues may require ID checks or basic health screenings, sex workers themselves are excluded from labor laws and social welfare systems, leaving many vulnerable to exploitation and abuse.

Penalties under the law vary significantly. Adult sex workers may be fined up to **1,000 THB (approximately $27 USD)** for engaging in prostitution, while those found soliciting in public or working in unauthorized venues may face short-term detention or additional fines. While this may not seem high by Western standards, it represents a significant financial burden in Thailand, where the minimum daily wage is around 330 THB (about $9 USD) and many workers earn far less. However, much harsher penalties apply to those managing brothels, trafficking individuals, or engaging in sex with minors—including prison sentences of **10 to 20 years** and fines of several **thousand baht**. Foreign nationals involved in prostitution—whether as clients or operators—can be **deported, imprisoned**, and **permanently blacklisted** from reentering Thailand. While enforcement can appear lax, especially in tourist-heavy areas, the legal risks remain substantial, particularly when minors or trafficking are involved.

Prostitution Practices

Prostitution in Thailand, though officially outlawed, remains **widespread** and often **operates in plain sight**. Estimates from UNAIDS in 2014 suggested that over 120,000 people were involved in sex work across the country, though some NGOs and researchers believe the real number could exceed 300,000 when accounting for informal workers. The industry contributes significantly to the local economies of tourist-heavy cities like **Bangkok, Pattaya**, and **Phuket**, where the line between entertainment and sex work is often blurred.

Despite legal restrictions, sex work continues in many forms, including **bar-based work** in go-go and beer bars, **massage parlors** offering discreet services, and **street-based** or freelance sex work conducted through nightlife zones, social media, or dating apps. **Escort services** and **private arrangements**—often conducted through websites or encrypted messaging apps—are also increasingly popular, especially with foreign visitors. Many "entertainment venues," such as bathhouses or karaoke bars, operate under ambiguous legal status, offering sexual services under the guise of hospitality or companionship.

For tourists, it's crucial to understand the legal and ethical risks involved. While prostitution may appear tolerated or normalized in certain areas, participating in it is still **technically illegal**, and authorities do occasionally conduct raids or sting operations—especially in response to international scrutiny or human trafficking concerns. Engaging in prostitution with a minor (under 18) carries severe penalties, including **up to 20 years in prison**, regardless of whether the individual presented fake documents or claimed to be of age. Foreigners found guilty of such offenses may face not only lengthy imprisonment but also **deportation and permanent blacklisting** from Thailand. Additionally, many sex workers operate in precarious situations, often lacking legal protection or healthcare access, and may be under coercion or trafficking. Tourists should be cautious, respectful, and aware of the complex human rights issues surrounding the sex trade. What may seem like a harmless or normalized part of the tourism scene could carry serious legal and moral consequences.

Sex Trafficking and Exploitation

Sex trafficking and sexual exploitation remain **serious human rights concerns** in Thailand, despite the country's modern infrastructure and international reputation as a tourist destination. Thailand is both a source and destination country for trafficking victims. Several factors contribute to the scale of the problem: widespread poverty in rural areas, especially in the north and northeast; a demand-driven commercial sex industry; porous borders with neighboring countries like Myanmar, Laos, and Cambodia; and inadequate labor protections. Traffickers often lure individuals with promises of legitimate employment, then coerce or force them into sex work, stripping them of freedom and legal recourse. Migrants, stateless persons, and impoverished Thais—especially women and children—are particularly vulnerable. While the sex industry itself is largely tolerated, the illegal nature of prostitution leaves workers with limited access to justice or protection, making them easy targets for exploitation.

Certain regions of Thailand are more affected than others. Border provinces such as **Chiang Rai, Tak**, and **Mukdahan** are major transit and recruitment zones, particularly for migrants from Myanmar and Laos. Urban centers like **Bangkok, Pattaya**, and **Phuket** are common destinations where victims are trafficked into the entertainment and sex trade. The most at-risk demographics include underage girls, LGBTQ+ youth, ethnic minorities, undocumented migrants, and those with limited education or economic opportunity. The Thai government has made strides in recent years, establishing anti-trafficking units, passing stricter laws like the **Anti-Trafficking in Persons Act B.E. 2551 (2008)**, and partnering with NGOs and international agencies. However, enforcement remains uneven, and corruption can hinder investigations and prosecutions. NGOs report that victims are often treated as criminals rather than as individuals in need of protection. While awareness and political will are growing, experts agree that a more coordinated effort—focused on prevention, victim support, and accountability—is still needed to address trafficking at its roots.

 ## Sex Tourism and Public Health

Sex tourism is definitely present in Thailand and has been a notable part of the country's tourism landscape for many years. Popular destinations for sex tourism include Bangkok, especially areas like **Patpong, Nana Plaza**, and **Soi Cowboy**, as well as **Pattaya** and **Phuket**, which attract many tourists seeking nightlife and adult entertainment. **Chiang Mai** and some smaller resort towns also see sex tourism activity, though to a lesser extent.

The organization and advertisement of sex tourism in Thailand operate through a mix of visible and discreet channels. Online platforms such as websites and social media promote venues and services, often catering to foreign tourists. Local brothels, bars, and massage parlors openly target sex tourists, sometimes employing staff fluent in multiple languages. Travel agencies occasionally include nightlife and adult entertainment in their packages, while printed and digital guides, as well as word-of-mouth recommendations, help tourists navigate the scene. Advertising is often subtle, with neon signs and flyers, but online ads also play a significant role. Public health concerns related to sex tourism in Thailand are considerable.

The country has faced challenges with **HIV/AIDS** and other **sexually transmitted infections (STIs)**, and sex tourism can increase the risk of transmission through unprotected sex and multiple partners. Aside from HIV, other STIs such as gonorrhea, syphilis, and chlamydia are prevalent among some sex worker populations. **Drug use**, sometimes linked to nightlife and the sex industry, adds another layer of public health complexity. **Exploitation** and **human trafficking** are deeply intertwined issues, which not only raise ethical and legal concerns but also create barriers to healthcare access for vulnerable individuals involved in the sex trade. These populations often face stigma and legal risks that limit their ability to seek treatment. **Mental health problems** such as trauma and stress are also significant among sex workers and some tourists. Thailand has launched various public health interventions, including condom distribution and health education programs, but despite these efforts, many challenges remain in fully addressing the health risks associated with sex tourism.

 ## Tips to Avoid Being Solicited

If you want to avoid being solicited while traveling in Thailand, it's important to stay cautious and choose your locations carefully. Here are some practical tips to help you steer clear of unwanted attention:

- Avoid nightlife areas known for sex tourism, such as Patpong in Bangkok, Walking Street in Pattaya, and certain spots in Phuket.

- Stick to family-friendly or cultural neighborhoods and popular tourist attractions.

- Dress modestly and act respectfully to minimize attracting attention.

- Politely but firmly say no if approached with offers or invitations that make you uncomfortable.

- Don't accept drinks or invitations from strangers in bars or clubs.

- Use trusted sources like hotel staff or official guides for recommendations on places to visit.

- If you are propositioned, respond firmly but politely with a clear "no," and then walk away without engaging further to avoid escalation or misunderstandings.

 ## Law of the Land True Story

In August 2023, a significant case involving an American tourist and prostitution in Thailand came to light. A 48-year-old American man, referred to as "Bass," and his 34-year-old Thai girlfriend, Kanya, were arrested for allegedly operating a large-scale online escort service that catered to foreign tourists. The operation was based in Hua Hin, a popular resort city in Prachuap Khiri Khan province. The couple faced charges related to prostitution offenses, including providing services catering to the desires of others and assisting, facilitating, or protecting the operation of prostitution by others.

The couple's website, Absolute Angels Bangkok, was reportedly the most visited of its kind in Thailand, attracting nearly 430,000 visits per month. The site offered a range of services provided by women, transgender individuals, and groups of sex workers working in pairs. It included detailed descriptions and photographs of each sex worker, along with "customer reviews" written by English-speaking foreigners. The website operated across various popular tourist destinations in Thailand, including Bangkok, Pattaya, Phuket, Chiang Mai, and Hua Hin.

The operation came under scrutiny after foreign tourists reported being drugged and robbed by Thai prostitutes sent through the Absolute Angels Bangkok website. An investigation revealed that the website openly offered prostitution services to foreign tourists, leading to the arrests of the couple and the seizure of assets worth over 40 million baht (about $1.15 million USD), including a pool villa, luxury cars, and bank accounts containing 9 million baht (about $260,000 USD).

 **Takeaways**

- Although prostitution is officially illegal in Thailand, it remains a large and highly visible part of the economy and tourism industry, operating openly in many areas despite uneven law enforcement.

- The legal framework criminalizes prostitution-related activities with varying penalties, but sex workers themselves have no formal labor protections, leaving many vulnerable to exploitation, abuse, and lack of healthcare access.

- Sex trafficking and exploitation are serious ongoing problems in Thailand, fueled by poverty, migration, porous borders, and demand for commercial sex, with vulnerable groups including women, children, migrants, and minorities.

- Sex tourism is concentrated in well-known nightlife districts and promoted through both overt and discreet channels, raising significant public health concerns such as the spread of HIV/STIs, drug use, and mental health issues among sex workers and tourists.

- Travelers can reduce the risk of being solicited by avoiding known red-light districts, sticking to family-friendly areas, dressing modestly, declining offers firmly, and relying on trusted local guidance to navigate safely.

LGBTQ

CHAPTER 8

LGBTQ

Homophobia in Thailand

Thailand is often perceived internationally as a relatively **LGBTQ+-friendly country**, especially compared to its regional neighbors. It is known for its vibrant LGBTQ+ communities, especially in urban areas like Bangkok, Chiang Mai, and Pattaya. **Same-sex relationships** are **legal**, and transgender individuals (known locally as kathoey or "ladyboys") are highly visible in media, entertainment, and everyday life. However, this apparent openness can obscure the deeper, more systemic forms of homophobia and discrimination that persist beneath the surface.

While societal tolerance exists, true acceptance and equal treatment are far from guaranteed. **Homophobic attitudes remain prevalent** in many areas of Thai society, particularly in rural regions and within traditional families. LGBTQ+ individuals often face pressure to conform to heteronormative expectations, including marriage and gender roles. Many LGBTQ+ Thais experience stigma, bullying, or rejection from family members, especially during adolescence. Mental health struggles, including depression and suicide, are reported at higher rates among LGBTQ+ youth due to social isolation and discrimination.

Institutionally, legal protections for LGBTQ+ individuals in Thailand have recently improved significantly, but challenges remain. Same-sex marriage is now legal as of January 2025, although other protections—especially for transgender and gender-diverse people—are still partial or unevenly enforced.

In schools, LGBTQ+ students frequently encounter harassment and a lack of support. Education policies do not mandate inclusive sex education or LGBTQ+ representation, and many teachers are unprepared to address issues of gender and sexual diversity. Moreover, traditional values rooted in Buddhism and conservative cultural norms can contribute to silent disapproval or passive exclusion, even when overt hostility is absent.

Thus, while Thailand presents a tolerant image and offers more visibility and informal freedom than many countries in the region, underlying homophobia remains a significant concern. True equality for LGBTQ+ people in Thailand will require not only social progress but also legal reform, comprehensive education, and cultural shifts toward genuine inclusion and protection.

LGBTQ Legislation

LGBTQ legislation in Thailand has made significant strides in recent years, culminating in the legalization of same-sex marriage. **As of January 23, 2025, same-sex couples can legally marry in Thailand**, making it the first country in Southeast Asia to pass marriage equality into law. This came after the **Marriage Equality Act** was passed by Parliament and received royal assent in September 2024. The law amended dozens of sections in the Civil and Commercial Code, replacing gender-specific terms with gender-neutral ones, thereby granting same-sex spouses the same legal rights and responsibilities as opposite-sex couples. These include inheritance rights, medical decision-making authority, joint property ownership, and adoption rights. The implementation process involved updating government systems and training staff across provincial and district offices to accommodate same-sex marriage registrations. On the first day of legal marriage, over 1,800 same-sex couples registered their unions, a milestone that highlighted widespread enthusiasm and media attention.[9]

---

9   https://apnews.com/article/
    thailand-lgbtq-marriage-law-c2162f07cd103ea86631a137d6b6d193

The economic impact of this legislative shift is also noteworthy. Analysts predict that legalizing same-sex marriage will boost Thailand's economy by up to $2 billion in tourism revenue and create more than 150,000 new jobs.[10] LGBTQ travelers already regard Thailand as a welcoming destination, and this legal reform strengthens its reputation as a leader in LGBTQ rights in Asia. However, while marriage equality is a historic step, other legal protections remain underdeveloped. Thailand still **does not allow individuals to change their gender marker** on official documents, as the proposed Gender Recognition Bill was rejected in early 2024. Transgender individuals continue to face legal and administrative hurdles in accessing healthcare, employment, and social services. Additionally, an Anti-Discrimination Bill that would provide legal protections based on sexual orientation and gender identity is still under review. Without these measures, many LGBTQ individuals remain vulnerable to bias in schools, workplaces, and public institutions.

Despite its progressive image, Thailand's LGBTQ community continues to face challenges rooted in social stigma and legal gaps. Traditional gender roles and family expectations often marginalize non-conforming individuals, and rural areas in particular tend to be less accepting. Legal reform, while essential, must be accompanied by cultural and educational shifts to ensure that equality is realized not only in law but in everyday life. Nevertheless, Thailand's move to legalize same-sex marriage marks a significant turning point and reflects growing public support and political will to advance LGBTQ rights in the country.

LGBTQ Tourism and Safety Concerns

LGBTQ tourism **is highly developed** in Thailand. The country has long marketed itself as a welcoming destination for LGBTQ travelers, bolstered by its vibrant nightlife, inclusive culture, and progressive legislation such as the recent legalization of same-sex marriage. Campaigns like **"Go Thai Be Free"** and upcoming events like **World Pride 2028** highlight Thailand's intent to become a global hub for LGBTQ tourism. LGBTQ travelers—particularly from Western countries and East

---

10   https://en.wikipedia.org/wiki/Marriage_Equality_Act_%28Thailand%29

Asia—frequent destinations like Bangkok, Phuket, Pattaya, and Chiang Mai for their gay-friendly accommodations, festivals, and nightlife. Travel agencies and businesses often cater specifically to LGBTQ clientele, and the Tourism Authority of Thailand actively promotes inclusivity in its global marketing efforts.

Tolerance toward LGBTQ individuals **varies by region.** Urban centers such as Bangkok, Pattaya, Phuket, and Chiang Mai are very LGBTQ-friendly, offering a wide range of queer bars, clubs, pride events, and LGBTQ-owned businesses. These areas also tend to have higher visibility and acceptance of diverse gender identities and sexual orientations. In contrast, rural provinces and conservative communities may be less accepting, where traditional cultural norms dominate and LGBTQ individuals may face social stigma or misunderstanding. That said, overt hostility or violence is rare, and general politeness in Thai society helps mitigate uncomfortable interactions.

Public displays of affection between LGBTQ visitors are **generally tolerated in major tourist hubs, though they should be kept modest.** Thai culture—regardless of sexual orientation—tends to be **conservative in public behavior.** Holding hands or subtle gestures are usually acceptable in places like Bangkok or Phuket, but kissing or overt intimacy may draw unwanted attention or disapproval, especially in more traditional or rural settings.

Regarding safety, Thailand is considered **one of the safest countries in Asia for LGBTQ travelers.** Violent homophobic or transphobic incidents are rare, especially in areas popular with tourists. However, standard travel precautions still apply. LGBTQ visitors should be cautious of scams, drink spiking in nightlife districts, and petty theft. Transgender travelers may face challenges with official identification, as Thai law still does not allow individuals to change the gender marker on their ID cards. Additionally, while anti-discrimination laws exist, enforcement is inconsistent, and LGBTQ individuals—especially locals—may face workplace or housing discrimination. Overall, with cultural awareness and basic safety precautions, LGBTQ travelers can enjoy Thailand safely and confidently.

General Questions

1. *Do laws in Thailand protect homosexual expressions and conduct?* **Yes.** Laws in Thailand protect homosexual expression and conduct. Same-sex activity has been legal since 1956, and the 2015 Gender Equality Act prohibits discrimination based on sexual orientation or gender identity. In January 2025, Thailand became the first Southeast Asian country to legalize same-sex marriage, granting equal rights to same-sex couples. However, challenges remain.

2. *Are LGBTQ tourists in Thailand likely to face discrimination or challenges when booking accommodations, accessing services, or engaging in public activities?* **No.** LGBTQ tourists in Thailand generally face minimal discrimination when booking accommodations, accessing services, or participating in public activities, especially in popular tourist areas like Bangkok, Phuket, Pattaya, and Chiang Mai. These cities are known for their welcoming atmosphere, inclusive businesses, and vibrant LGBTQ nightlife. Many hotels and resorts actively market themselves as LGBTQ-friendly, and staff are typically respectful and professional. However, in more rural or conservative regions, travelers may encounter occasional discomfort or subtle bias, particularly toward same-sex couples showing affection publicly. While overt discrimination is rare, LGBTQ visitors are still advised to remain culturally aware, exercise discretion in public displays of affection, and choose LGBTQ-welcoming establishments to ensure a safe and respectful experience.

Law of the Land Hypothetical

HYPOTHETICAL: *Alex, an American tourist visiting Thailand, recently married his Thai same-sex partner under the new Marriage Equality*

Act. They want to adopt a child while living in Thailand. However, Alex's partner is a transgender woman who has not legally changed her gender on official documents Under Thailand's current laws, can a same-sex couple—where one partner is transgender but has not legally changed gender markers—legally adopt a child? How does the legal status of transgender individuals affect family rights such as adoption in Thailand?

ANSWER: *While Thailand has legalized same-sex marriage, adoption laws remain unclear and less inclusive. Since the transgender partner has not legally changed her gender on official documents, this can complicate adoption applications and parental recognition. Courts often rely on traditional definitions of family, which may pose challenges for same-sex couples and transgender individuals without legal gender recognition. Although the marriage is valid, adopting as a same-sex couple with a transgender partner lacking legal gender change involves significant legal hurdles. Couples in this situation usually need legal advice and may face complex court processes.*

SEXUALLY MOTIVATED/ VIOLENT CRIMES

CHAPTER 9
SEXUALLY MOTIVATED/ VIOLENT CRIMES

Overview

Sexually motivated crimes in Thailand are a recognized issue, though their exact prevalence can be difficult to assess due to underreporting, social stigma, and legal obstacles. These crimes include sexual assault, harassment, and trafficking, and they affect both Thai citizens and foreigners. While Thailand is **generally considered safe** for both travelers and residents, it has also been identified as a source, destination, and transit country for human trafficking, particularly for sexual exploitation. Law enforcement and non-governmental organizations have made efforts to combat these crimes, but cultural attitudes and limited resources sometimes hinder progress.

The most affected population tends to be women and children, especially those from economically disadvantaged or marginalized backgrounds. Migrant workers, ethnic minorities, and individuals from rural provinces are particularly vulnerable due to lack of education, financial pressure, and limited legal protection. Children are at heightened risk in cases of exploitation and trafficking, particularly in the context of sex tourism—an issue Thailand has long struggled to address, despite tougher laws and international scrutiny.

Regionally, urban centers and tourist-heavy areas like **Bangkok, Pattaya, Phuket**, and **Chiang Mai** see higher reported rates of sexually motivated crimes, partly due to their larger populations and the presence of night-life and entertainment industries. Rural and border provinces, such as those near **Myanmar**, **Laos**, and **Cambodia**, may also see elevated rates due to trafficking routes and weaker enforcement. However, the true scale of regional variation is hard to quantify due to differing levels of reporting and access to justice.

Related Legislation

Thailand has made significant strides in developing legal protections and penalties for sexually motivated crimes, particularly in response to domestic challenges and international pressure. At the heart of this framework is the **Thai Criminal Code**, which outlines various sexual offenses, including rape, harassment, and exploitation of minors. For example, rape is punishable by **up to 20 years** in prison—or life in particularly severe cases, such as those involving children or weapons. In a landmark shift, Thailand criminalized **marital rape** in 2007, a move that reflected changing social attitudes toward consent and bodily autonomy within marriage. Other provisions in the Penal Code apply harsher penalties when the victims are children, or when there is use of force or coercion.

Beyond the Criminal Code, Thailand's **Anti-Trafficking in Persons Act of 2008** serves as a major legal weapon against trafficking for sexual purposes. This law not only imposes **heavy prison sentences and fines on traffickers**, but also provides for **victim support services**, such as shelter, legal aid, and even temporary residency for non-Thai victims. Complementing this, the **Child Protection Act of 2003** offers a legal basis for safeguarding minors from abuse and exploitation, both offline and online. In recent years, Thailand has also turned its attention to digital crimes through the **Computer Crime Act**, which addresses issues like cyber-harassment and the distribution of child sexual abuse material.

Thailand's laws on sexually motivated crimes apply **equally to visitors and Thai citizens**. Any person within Thai borders—whether resident or tourist—is subject to the country's criminal laws, including those governing rape, sexual harassment, exploitation, and trafficking. Foreign nationals who commit such offenses can be arrested, tried, and sentenced under Thai law, facing serious penalties that may include long prison terms, substantial fines, and in some cases, life imprisonment. Once a sentence is served, foreigners are often deported and blacklisted from re-entering the country.

Thailand has worked in recent years to distance itself from its historical association with sex tourism, and laws targeting offenses such as child exploitation and trafficking are enforced regardless of the perpetrator's nationality. Foreigners involved in sex crimes against children, in particular, face especially harsh penalties under Thai law, and many are prosecuted in cooperation with international law enforcement agencies. In some cases, their home countries may also pursue charges upon their return, particularly in jurisdictions with extraterritorial laws covering crimes like child sexual abuse committed abroad.

At the same time, foreign visitors who become victims of sexual crimes in Thailand are entitled to legal protection and support. Although reporting and follow-up procedures can be complicated by language barriers or unfamiliar legal processes, mechanisms exist for victims to access medical care, safe housing, and legal aid. In high-profile or severe cases, embassies and international organizations often work alongside Thai authorities to ensure that foreign victims receive appropriate assistance and that justice is pursued through the local legal system.

Despite these robust legal instruments, enforcement remains a persistent challenge. Victims—especially women, children, and migrants—often hesitate to come forward due to fear of retaliation, shame, or a lack of faith in the justice system. In some cases, corruption within law enforcement and weak investigative capacity further hamper justice. However, Thailand has shown a growing willingness to engage with international organizations and improve institutional capacity, creating **special police divisions** and partnering with global agencies to strengthen investigations and victim support. Still, translating strong laws into meaningful protection on the ground remains a work in progress.

 **General Questions**

1. *Do laws in Thailand related to sex crimes protect the victims equally?* **Yes.** Thai laws related to sex crimes are designed to protect all victims equally, regardless of gender, age, or nationality. In theory, **legal protections apply universally**, with provisions for support services, justice, and safety. However, in practice, equal protection is not always realized. Victims from marginalized groups—such as migrants, sex workers, or ethnic minorities—often face barriers like stigma, fear, language issues, or distrust of authorities. Foreign victims may also struggle with legal procedures or visa concerns. While the legal framework is strong, enforcement remains inconsistent, and vulnerable individuals may not always receive the protection they are entitled to.

2. *Pursuant to law, what is the age of consent for sex in Thailand?* The legal age of consent for sex in Thailand is **15 years old.** Sexual activity with anyone under 15 is considered statutory rape, regardless of consent. While those aged 15 to 17 can legally consent, such cases may still lead to legal action if a complaint is filed by the minor or their guardian.

 **Law of the Land True Story**[11]

In February 2025, Immigration Police Division 3 arrested two Swiss nationals in Pattaya for sexual offenses against minors. The first suspect, Mr. Rudolf, age 68, collaborated with a Thai accomplice to contact the guardian of a girl in Surat Thani province, requesting to adopt her and offering to fund her education at a school in Chonburi

---

11   https://www.khaosodenglish.com/news/2025/02/19/
     pattaya-police-arrest-two-swiss-men-in-separate-child-sex-abuse-cases

province. The guardian, believing it would benefit the child, allowed her to live with Mr. Rudolf.

Later, Pattaya Police received complaints about his sexual abuse of the child. After investigation, they obtained a search warrant for his residence, where they found external hard drives and flash drives containing explicit photos and videos of the girl in various situations, including bathing. During questioning, the girl confirmed she was molested and forced to pose in various ways, with the suspect using intimidation when she refused. On February 18, Pattaya Police arrested and charged Mr. Rudolf with possession of child pornography for sexual exploitation and committing indecent acts against a child under 13 years old, regardless of consent, using coercion against a person under his authority. He was initially granted bail but fled before sentencing. Immigration officers and Pattaya Police later found him hiding in an apartment in Nongprue, Banglamung, Chonburi, and arrested him.

The second suspect, Mr. Oliver, age 41, entered Thailand as a tourist in April 2023. He used the Tinder application to solicit sexual services from a Thai female minor under 15 years old. He fled before being prosecuted. However, when he re-entered Thailand in February 2025, he tried to evade arrest by hiding in a hotel in Nongprue, Banglamung, Chonburi. Nevertheless, he was arrested by the Immigration Investigation Division officers, and the Chonburi Provincial Court immediately issued an arrest warrant.

Police Major General Chairit Anurut, Commander of Immigration Division 3, stated that authorities prioritize foreign nationals' criminal cases, especially sexual offenses, noting that victims of such crimes suffer tremendously. He explained that the two cases differ in detail – the first suspect clearly used financial status as a means to access the victim, while the second claimed the victim was willing and that he was unaware of her true age. He warned tourists using dating apps to be cautious.

 **Takeaways**

- Sexually motivated crimes affect mainly women and children, especially those from marginalized backgrounds such as migrant workers, ethnic minorities, and rural populations. These groups face heightened risks due to economic hardship, lack of education, and limited legal protection.

- Urban and tourist-heavy areas like Bangkok, Pattaya, Phuket, and Chiang Mai report higher rates of sexual crimes, influenced by larger populations and entertainment industries. Border provinces also face challenges due to trafficking routes, though exact regional differences are hard to measure because of underreporting.

- Thailand has comprehensive laws against sexual offenses, including rape (punishable by up to 20 years or life imprisonment), child exploitation, trafficking, and cyber-related crimes. Landmark changes like criminalizing marital rape in 2007 show evolving attitudes toward consent.

- Thai sexual crime laws apply equally to citizens and foreigners. Foreign offenders can face long prison terms, fines, deportation, and blacklisting. The government actively prosecutes foreign nationals involved in such crimes, cooperating with international agencies when necessary.

- Victims, including foreigners, are entitled to legal protection, medical care, and support services. However, language barriers, social stigma, and sometimes corruption or weak enforcement can limit victims' access to justice and protection.

-

ARRESTED IN THAILAND

ARRESTED IN THAILAND

Overview

When traveling in a foreign country, it's imperative to recognize that you are subject to the legal jurisdiction and regulations of that nation. These laws may significantly differ from those in your home country and might not offer the same legal protections you are accustomed to. It's crucial to bear in mind that penalties for violating foreign laws can be more severe than those for similar offenses in your home country, and ignorance of these laws is not typically accepted as a defense.

The consequences for breaking the law while abroad can be severe and may include expulsion, fines, arrest, or imprisonment. Even unintentional violations can lead to serious legal repercussions. It is essential for travelers to be aware of and adhere to the laws of the host country to avoid legal entanglements and ensure a safe and enjoyable experience.

Specifically, stringent penalties are often enforced for possession, use, or trafficking of illegal drugs in many countries. Convicted offenders can expect severe consequences, including lengthy jail sentences and hefty fines. The legal processes for foreigners in the event of an arrest abroad involve being charged or indicted, prosecuted, potentially convicted and sentenced, and, if applicable, going through an appeals process.

Navigating a foreign legal system can be complex, and individuals arrested abroad must be prepared to comply with the legal procedures of the host country. Seeking legal representation and understanding the local legal nuances are crucial steps for those facing legal issues in a foreign jurisdiction.

Awareness of and adherence to the laws of a foreign country are paramount when traveling. Understanding the potential consequences for legal violations and being prepared to navigate the legal system of the host country are essential aspects of responsible international travel.

Arrest Process

In Thailand, the arrest process generally begins when the police have reasonable grounds to suspect someone has committed a crime. Upon arrest, the individual must be informed of the charges and their rights, including the right to remain silent and the right to legal counsel. The police are required to bring the arrested person before a court **within 48 hours** for a judicial hearing to determine whether to grant bail or continue detention.

For foreigners, there are some **special considerations**. Thai authorities typically notify the foreign embassy or consulate soon after the arrest to ensure consular assistance is available. Language barriers can be a significant issue, so interpreters are often provided during questioning and legal proceedings to ensure the foreigner understands the process. Foreign nationals also have the right to legal representation, but they must arrange their own lawyer or seek help from their embassy.

Additionally, foreigners accused of serious crimes, especially sexually motivated offenses, may face stricter scrutiny and often remain in custody throughout the investigation and trial. Once convicted, foreigners usually serve their sentences in Thai prisons and, upon release, are commonly deported and banned from re-entry. Throughout the process, embassies often assist with communication, legal advice, and ensuring fair treatment under Thai law.

Rights of the Arrested Person

Under Thai law, anyone who is arrested—whether a Thai citizen or a foreign traveler—has specific rights designed to protect them during the arrest and legal process. These rights include being **informed promptly of the reason for their arrest, the right to remain silent to avoid self-incrimination**, and the **right to legal counsel**. The arrested individual must be brought before a court **within 48 hours** for a hearing to decide on detention or bail.

For foreign travelers, these rights remain the same in principle, but there are additional safeguards. Thai authorities are required to notify the detainee's embassy or consulate without delay, ensuring the foreigner has access to **consular assistance**. This assistance can include help with finding a lawyer, translation services, and ensuring fair treatment. Foreigners have the right to an interpreter during police questioning and court proceedings, though in practice, access to quality interpretation may vary.

Both Thai nationals and foreigners have the right to legal representation, though foreigners often rely on embassy resources or private lawyers familiar with international cases. Despite these protections, foreign travelers may face practical challenges such as language barriers, unfamiliarity with the Thai legal system, and sometimes limited access to their preferred legal counsel. Nonetheless, the fundamental rights to be informed, to remain silent, to legal defense, and to a timely court appearance are guaranteed by Thai law for all arrested individuals.

Getting Legal Assistance

If you are arrested in Thailand, the most direct sources of help are the **Lawyers Council of Thailand**, which operates a Legal Aid Center in Bangkok. (For more information, please visit **www.lawyerscouncil.or.th**), and the nationwide **Tourist Police hotline at 1155**, which runs 24/7 and can connect foreigners with interpreters or legal contacts. Foreign nationals should also request immediate contact with their

embassy; while embassies cannot interfere in Thai proceedings, they maintain lists of English-speaking lawyers and will ensure fair treatment.

In Bangkok, **Tilleke & Gibbins**[12] is one of Thailand's largest and most respected law firms, with experience in criminal defense, civil litigation, and business law. They are widely recommended for foreigners needing reliable representation. **Siam Legal International**[13] operates in Bangkok, Chiang Mai, Pattaya, and Phuket. The firm focuses on serving international clients, handling criminal cases, family law, visa issues, and civil disputes. Another established option is **Chaninat & Leeds**[14], a Bangkok-based firm staffed by both U.S. and Thai attorneys. They specialize in criminal defense, family law, and business matters, offering fully bilingual services for foreign nationals.

Bail

Thailand operates a bail system, governed primarily by the Criminal Procedure Code, which enables suspects—including both Thai nationals and foreign visitors—to secure release while awaiting trial. Under Thai law, bail (or a bail bond) may take the form of **cash, property, or third-party surety**, all intended to guarantee the accused's return for court proceedings. A bail application must be formally submitted to the court, which evaluates factors such as the nature and seriousness of the alleged crime, strength of evidence, risk of flight, ties to the community, and any potential harm to victims or witnesses before making a decision.

Where bail is **granted**, the accused (or their guarantor) must provide the required security—whether cash, property deeds, or a surety agreement—to the court. In cases where bail **is contested** by the prosecution or police, a hearing may be held before the judge grants release and sets conditions such as surrendering a passport, regular check-ins with authorities, or restrictions on contact with witnesses.

---

12   www.tilleke.com

13   www.siam-legal.com

14   www.thailand-lawyer.com

While Thailand does not formally set minimum bail amounts in law, many offenses have **preset bail levels** that provide a guideline—though judges retain the discretion to adjust amounts. Bail amounts vary widely based on the nature of the alleged crime. For minor offenses, bail may range from 30,000 to 100,000 THB (approximately $850 to $2,800 USD). For more serious charges—such as drug offenses, child exploitation, or violent crimes—bail can be set much higher, sometimes between 200,000 to over 1,000,000 THB (around $5,600 to over $28,000 USD). In capital cases or where the court believes there's a strong flight risk, bail may be denied altogether.[15]

Foreign visitors are eligible for bail, but courts often consider them flight risks, so they may face **stricter conditions**. These may include higher bail amounts, property-based bail rather than cash, and surrender of travel documents or passports. Visa status and immigration concerns may further complicate the process. Bail is less likely for serious crimes like those involving minors or drug trafficking. If bail is granted, the court issues a **receipt**. The security is refunded if the accused complies with bail conditions and attends all hearings. Violation can result in revocation of bail, forfeiture of deposits, and arrest warrants being issued.

In essence, Thailand's bail system does allow pretrial release for most individuals, including foreigners. However, especially for non-citizens, the process may be more stringent and challenging—making legal representation essential to navigate the nuanced and discretionary judicial process.

Complaints Against Police

The general reputation of the police force in Thailand is mixed. While many Thai police officers perform their duties professionally and diligently, the institution has long faced criticism for corruption, lack of transparency, and selective enforcement of the law. Among locals and foreign nationals alike, there is a perception that bribery, abuse of power, and inefficiency can be widespread, particularly in cases involving minor

---

15   https://www.thailandbail.com

offenses, traffic stops, or immigration checks. High-profile scandals and inconsistent accountability have contributed to a public trust deficit, though recent government efforts have sought to reform the force and improve its public image.

For foreign visitors, the most common complaints about the Thai police often involve allegations of **extortion, arbitrary or selective enforcement**, and **unclear procedures following arrests or detentions.** Tourists have reported being stopped and searched without cause, especially in nightlife areas or high-tourism zones like Pattaya, Phuket, and Bangkok. Other complaints include delays in handling cases where the foreigner is a victim, poor communication due to language barriers, and a lack of clear guidance on rights during detention. In some cases, foreigners have felt pressured into paying unofficial fines to avoid further complications.

In Thailand, individuals who wish to report police misconduct have several official avenues available, depending on the nature and seriousness of the complaint. Complaints can be submitted directly to the **local police station** where the incident occurred, but for cases involving serious misconduct or a conflict of interest, it's advisable to contact the **Royal Thai Police headquarters** in Bangkok or file through the **Office of the Inspector General**. Complaints can also be submitted online via the Royal Thai Police website at **https://www.royalthaipolice.go.th.** Additionally, embassies often assist their citizens in navigating the complaint process, and international visitors are encouraged to involve their consulate early if they experience abuse or irregular treatment. Tourists or visitors dealing with less serious issues may also reach out to the **Tourist Police,** who are accessible by phone at 1155 or in person at local branches. However, for more systemic or serious misconduct, it is generally more effective to direct complaints to the national watchdog agencies such as the **Office of the Ombudsman, the National Human Rights Commission (NHRC)**, or the **National Anti-Corruption Commission (NACC)**. The Ombudsman deals with instances of administrative wrongdoing or unfair treatment by police, the NHRC focuses on human rights violations, and the NACC investigates corruption and abuse of power. Complaints to these agencies can typically be filed in person, by mail, or online—with the NACC also accepting reports by phone.

When preparing to file a complaint, it is important to stay calm and respectful during interactions with authorities. Gathering evidence such as photos, video recordings, or witness details can help strengthen a case. It is also advisable to keep detailed records of the incident, including dates, times, locations, and names of any officers involved. Seeking legal counsel—particularly from someone experienced in cases of police misconduct—can provide further guidance and improve the chances of a successful resolution.

 ## General Questions

1. *If I am convicted in Thailand, am I likely to be released on bail pending the outcome of my appeal?* In Thailand, being released on bail after a conviction is not automatic, but it is possible—especially if the convicted person files an appeal. The court has discretion to grant or deny bail based on several factors, such as the severity of the offense, the length of the sentence, the risk of flight, and whether the appeal appears to have merit. For serious crimes, particularly those involving violence or drugs, courts are less likely to grant bail after conviction. Foreign nationals may face additional scrutiny when applying for post-conviction bail due to the higher perceived flight risk. In such cases, the court may require a larger bail amount and more stringent conditions. If bail is granted, it typically comes with conditions such as surrendering a passport or remaining within the country.

2. *Who is entitled to bail?* In Thailand, anyone arrested or charged with a criminal offense—including foreign nationals—is entitled to apply for bail. However, bail is not automatically granted; the court considers factors like the seriousness of the crime, the suspect's history, flight risk, and public safety. While individuals accused of serious offenses can request bail, they often face higher amounts and stricter conditions. Bail rights apply at all stages, from arrest through trial and even after conviction during

an appeal, though it is commonly denied in severe cases such as murder or major drug crimes.

3. *If I am arrested, how soon will I see a judge or magistrate?* If you are arrested in Thailand, you are typically required by law to be brought before a judge or magistrate within 48 hours of your detention. This hearing is called the "detention hearing," where the judge reviews the legality of your arrest and decides whether to grant bail or continue holding you in custody. If the authorities fail to present you to a judge within this timeframe, your detention may be considered unlawful, and you could be released. However, in practice, delays can occur, especially in remote areas or during busy periods.

4. *Will I be able to contact my country's embassy in Thailand?* Yes. If you are arrested in Thailand, you have the right under international law, including the Vienna Convention on Consular Relations, to contact your country's embassy or consulate. You should inform the authorities as soon as possible so they can facilitate this communication. Embassies can provide various forms of support, such as helping you find a local lawyer, informing your family or friends, assisting with language barriers, and explaining your rights and the local legal system. While embassies cannot intervene directly in legal matters or provide legal representation, they play a vital role in ensuring you are treated fairly and that your rights are respected. It is recommended to have your embassy's contact information on hand when traveling in Thailand, and the Tourist Police can also assist in connecting you with your embassy if needed.

JAILS VS. PRISONS: CONDITIONS & CULTURE

JAILS VS. PRISONS: CONDITIONS & CULTURE

Overview

Thailand's prison system is managed by the **Department of Corrections under the Ministry of Justice** and includes a network of prisons and jails across the country. Prisons typically house inmates serving longer sentences after conviction, while jails are mainly used for individuals awaiting trial or serving shorter sentences. The system covers a wide range of facilities, from large central prisons to smaller provincial jails and detention centers. However, the system faces significant challenges, most notably **chronic overcrowding**. High incarceration rates combined with a slow judicial process contribute to a large number of detainees spending extended periods in pre-trial detention.

Beyond physical conditions, Thailand's prison system struggles with providing adequate healthcare, rehabilitation, and reintegration programs. Although some correctional facilities offer vocational training, education, and substance abuse treatment programs, these resources are often insufficient or inconsistently applied. Foreign inmates face additional hurdles, including language barriers, limited access to consular support, and difficulties understanding the local legal system. Despite these ongoing issues, the Thai government has acknowledged the need for reform and has been working with international organizations to improve prison conditions, reduce overcrowding, and expand rehabilitation efforts. The following sections will provide a more in-depth examination of these topics, including the rights of prisoners, conditions inside facilities, and ongoing reform initiatives.

Prison Conditions and Living Environment

Thailand's prison system is structured to accommodate a diverse inmate population, with facilities ranging from maximum-security prisons to minimum-security institutions. Prisons are typically classified **based on the severity of offenses committed**, with high-security facilities housing individuals convicted of serious crimes such as murder or drug trafficking. However, overcrowding remains a significant issue, with some prisons operating at over 300% capacity. This overcrowding leads to challenges in maintaining security classifications, as inmates may be housed together regardless of their risk levels.

Basic living conditions within Thai prisons are **often substandard.** Inmates typically receive simple meals that lack nutritional balance, and food quality can vary significantly between facilities. Sanitation facilities are often inadequate, leading to poor hygiene and increased health risks. Overcrowded conditions exacerbate these issues, making it difficult to maintain cleanliness and proper sanitation. Access to clean water is also a concern, with some reports indicating that water supply is limited or of poor quality.

The most glaring challenges facing Thailand's prison system include **severe overcrowding, inadequate healthcare, and insufficient access to basic needs.** The prison population has grown rapidly, with many facilities housing more inmates than their capacity allows. This overcrowding leads to cramped living conditions, limited access to healthcare, and increased tensions among inmates. Medical facilities within prisons are often under-resourced, and inmates may face delays in receiving necessary treatment.

In response to these challenges, the Thai government has initiated several reforms aimed at improving prison conditions. The **Prevention and Suppression of Torture and Enforced Disappearance Act,** enacted in 2023, criminalizes torture and enforced disappearances, introducing preventive measures and penalties for perpetrators.[16] Additionally, the Narcotics Code of 2021 emphasizes rehabilitation over incarceration for drug-related offenses, promoting patients' rehabilitation and social reintegration.[17] While these reforms are steps in the right direction, ongoing efforts are needed to address the systemic issues within the prison system.

Inmate Rights and Legal Protections

In Thailand, inmates retain certain legal rights under the country's Constitution and relevant laws, though the extent to which these rights are upheld in practice varies. The Thai Constitution recognizes the basic human dignity of all individuals, including prisoners, and provides protections against inhumane treatment. Inmates have the right to be treated with respect, to be protected from torture, and to access medical care. Furthermore, Thailand is a signatory to various international treaties, including the **Convention Against Torture**, which obligates the state to uphold standards of humane treatment in detention facilities.

Access to legal resources and the ability to appeal a court decision are core components of the justice process for inmates. Prisoners have the right to consult with legal counsel, and public defenders are provided to those who cannot afford private representation. Inmates can file appeals or seek a retrial, although the process may be lengthy and hampered by systemic delays, lack of legal awareness, or limited resources within the prison system. Some prisons also provide limited legal aid programs and library access for legal materials, but these are not uniformly available.

However, **issues of abuse**—whether physical, psychological, or administrative—remain a concern in Thai prisons. Reports from human rights organizations have highlighted cases of mistreatment, including overcrowding, neglect, and in some instances, violence by guards or other

---

16 https://www.icj.org/wp-content/uploads/2024/08/Prevention-and-Suppression-of-Torture-and-Enforced-Disappearance-Act-B.E.-2565.pdf

17 https://aseannarco.oncb.go.th/uploads/Ebook/pdf/1828893714663711.pdf

inmates. While prisoners theoretically have the right to file complaints through internal channels or external watchdog bodies like the **National Human Rights Commission**, fear of retaliation and a lack of trust in the complaint mechanisms often deter inmates from coming forward.

Efforts have been made to strengthen legal recourse and oversight, including the passage of the Prevention and Suppression of Torture and Enforced Disappearance Act, which criminalizes custodial abuse and provides channels for redress. Nonetheless, enforcement and accountability remain inconsistent, and ensuring that inmate rights are meaningfully protected continues to be a pressing challenge for the Thai penal system.

General Questions

1. *What is the difference between a jail and prison in Thailand?*
   In Thailand, the distinction between a jail and a prison generally aligns with differences in detention purpose and the length or stage of incarceration. A **jail**, often referred to as a **detention center** or **remand facility**, is primarily used for individuals who are awaiting trial or sentencing. These facilities also temporarily house those serving short-term sentences—usually less than one year—or those undergoing legal proceedings. On the other hand, a **prison** (or **correctional institution**) is designated for individuals who have been **convicted and sentenced** to longer terms. Prisons are typically more structured and may be classified by security level—such as minimum, medium, or maximum—based on the severity of the offense and the risk level of the inmates. While both types of facilities fall under the jurisdiction of the Department of Corrections, prisons are usually more permanent, while jails are more transitional in function.

2. *Do jails and prisons offer religious services to inmates?* Yes,
   but in limited capacity. While access to religious practice is
   constitutionally guaranteed in Thailand and many prisons **do
   provide access**—especially for Buddhism, which is the dominant religion, in practice, access to religious services for minority
   faiths such as Islam or Christianity can be **limited or inconsistent**, depending on the facility's location, resources, and staffing.
   So, while the policy supports religious freedom, actual implementation doesn't always meet that standard.

3. *How do prisoners spend their time?* In Thai prisons, inmates
   generally follow a strict daily routine that includes early wake-
   up calls, cleaning duties, and headcounts. Many prisoners are
   assigned to work programs such as manufacturing, agriculture,
   or facility maintenance, which are often mandatory and serve
   both disciplinary and rehabilitative purposes. Outside of work,
   inmates may have limited access to recreational activities like
   exercise, reading, or educational and vocational training, though
   overcrowding and resource constraints often restrict these
   opportunities. Religious services and behavior improvement
   programs are sometimes available, but not consistently offered
   across all facilities, leaving many inmates with long periods of
   idle time.

4. *How does the prison commissary system work in Thailand?*
   Thailand's prison commissary system allows inmates to buy
   approved items like food, toiletries, and water using funds held
   in a personal prison account, with a daily spending limit of about
   300 baht (roughly $8 USD). Inmates cannot use cash directly;
   purchases are made via fingerprint verification. Family or consular officials can deposit money into these accounts, often through
   designated banks like Krung Thai. Because government-provided
   meals and supplies are minimal—budgeted at just over $1 USD
   per day—the commissary is essential for supplementing basic
   needs. However, this system can also create inequality among
   inmates and has raised concerns over transparency and financial
   abuse, prompting efforts to modernize it.

5. ***What type of medical care do prisoners receive?*** Prisoners in Thailand are entitled to medical care under the Universal Healthcare Coverage (UC) scheme, which aims to provide equal access to healthcare services. In practice, however, the quality and availability of medical care in Thai prisons are frequently inadequate. Facilities are overcrowded, and the number of medical staff is insufficient to meet the needs of the inmate population. Common health issues among inmates include skin diseases, tuberculosis, and mental health disorders. While some prisons have initiated programs to improve healthcare, such as telemedicine services and collaborations with external hospitals, these efforts are not uniformly implemented across all facilities . Additionally, mental health care remains a significant concern, with a limited number of psychologists and psychiatrists available to address the needs of inmates.

6. ***What is prison culture in Thailand?*** Prison culture in Thailand is shaped by strict hierarchies, social dynamics, and unwritten rules that govern daily life among inmates. Respect for senior prisoners, often called "elders," plays a significant role in maintaining order, and newcomers are expected to navigate these social structures carefully. The culture is also influenced by gang affiliations and ethnic or regional backgrounds, which can affect an inmate's safety and status. Inmates often rely on informal networks for protection, access to resources, and information, as official support can be limited. Activities like work assignments, religious practices, and participation in prison-run programs help structure inmates' time and social interactions, but tensions and conflicts remain common due to overcrowding and resource scarcity. This complex social environment significantly impacts prisoners' well-being and rehabilitation opportunities.

CHAPTER 12

HELPING A FRIEND OR RELATIVE IMPRISONED IN THAILAND

HELPING A FRIEND OR RELATIVE IMPRISONED IN THAILAND

Overview

If your family member or friend is imprisoned while traveling in Thailand, it's important to stay calm and take immediate, informed action. The first step is to confirm the arrest. Try contacting them directly through phone, email, or messaging apps. If you can't reach them, call local police stations or detention centers in the area where they were last seen. If you're in Thailand, visiting the nearest police station in person may help locate them more quickly.

Once the arrest is confirmed, your next move should be to **contact your country's embassy or consulate** in Thailand. While embassies cannot intervene in legal proceedings or secure someone's release, they can provide essential support. This includes confirming your loved one's whereabouts, ensuring they are being treated fairly under Thai law, offering a list of local lawyers, and arranging for language translation if needed. Embassies also conduct welfare visits and can help notify the person's family back home, if you haven't already done so.

It's crucial to **hire a Thai criminal defense lawyer** as soon as possible. Legal proceedings in Thailand are conducted in Thai, and the justice system operates differently than in many Western countries. A qualified local attorney will help explain the charges, guide you through the court process, and determine whether bail is an option. In some cases, bail is allowed, but it depends on the seriousness of the charge and whether the authorities view the person as a flight risk. Understanding the specific charges is vital. Thailand has strict laws, particularly around drug possession, visa violations, public disorder, and offenses against the monarchy. Penalties can be severe, including long prison terms. A good lawyer will clarify the legal situation, the likely outcomes, and potential defenses.

Support your loved one while they are detained. Jail conditions in Thailand can be challenging, and detainees often rely on family and friends to provide essentials such as food, toiletries, or phone credit. Most detention centers allow visitation on certain days, though you may need to register and follow specific procedures. The legal process in Thailand can be lengthy, sometimes taking months or years. It's important to stay in regular contact with both the lawyer and the embassy to track progress. If your loved one is convicted, serving time in a Thai prison may be unavoidable, but there may be a chance later to request a transfer to a prison in their home country through a treaty, if one exists. Appeals and royal pardons are also possibilities in some cases, though they are not guaranteed and take time.

Throughout this process, having accurate contact details for key parties—such as the Thai prison, local lawyer, and embassy—will help you stay informed and involved. While the situation is undoubtedly stressful, knowing the steps and resources available can make a significant difference in protecting your friend or family member's rights and well-being.

Sending Food, Supplies, and Money to an Inmate

Sending food, supplies, and money to an inmate in a Thai prison is possible, but the process is regulated and varies depending on the prison. Thai correctional facilities generally allow families and friends to support inmates with basic necessities, especially since state-provided resources can be minimal. You should confirm the prison where your loved one is held. Each facility has its own visiting hours, rules, and procedures for delivering items. You'll usually need the inmate's full name, prison ID (if known), and case number to make any transaction or delivery.

To send **food**, prisons usually allow visitors to bring a limited quantity of cooked meals or snacks during scheduled visiting hours. However, food must meet **strict guidelines**—homemade meals might not be allowed, and all items are typically checked before being handed over. Many prisons have a designated canteen where friends and family can buy pre-approved food or hygiene items for inmates. Some even offer pre-packed care packages that can be purchased directly from the prison or online through authorized vendors.

When it comes to **supplies**, such as toiletries, clothing, or reading materials, each prison has restrictions. Basic items like soap, toothbrushes, toothpaste, feminine hygiene products, and underwear are usually accepted, but all packages are inspected for contraband. Electronic items, sharp objects, or anything that could be misused will be confiscated. It's best to call the prison directly or consult with a lawyer to confirm what's allowed.

Sending **money** is one of the most efficient ways to support an inmate. Funds can be deposited into an inmate's account at the prison, which they can use to buy food, toiletries, and other approved items from the prison canteen. This is especially important in Thai prisons, where daily essentials are not always adequately provided. Money can be sent in person at the prison or, in some cases, through bank transfer or mobile apps if the facility supports it. Many families use online transfer services like Western Union or MoneyGram, which offer international transfers to Thailand via bank deposit, card payment, or cash pickup. These services are generally reliable and convenient for getting money to the country quickly. Alternatively, you can arrange a direct bank transfer to the prisoner's account within the prison, if that's an option the facility supports. This requires detailed information, such as the inmate's full name, prison ID number, and specific transfer instructions provided by the prison. Some prisons also operate a store or internal account system that allows you to deposit money for the inmate to use on essentials like food and toiletries.

No matter which method you choose, it's important to contact the prison directly to confirm their current policies, acceptable forms of payment, and any specific requirements. **Thai prison regulations vary, and not all facilities accept every type of transfer.** Always keep a record of your transactions in case you need to verify the payment later. Proper preparation and communication with the prison can help ensure your support reaches your loved one safely and without delay.

Mail, Phone Calls, and Visitation

Staying in contact with a loved one in a Thai prison is possible through mail, phone calls, and in-person visits, though each method is governed by specific rules set by the individual facility. Communication can be a lifeline for both the inmate and their family, but it requires careful planning and adherence to prison regulations.

Mail is often the most reliable and consistent way to stay in touch. Letters should be written clearly and respectfully, avoiding any content that could be seen as sensitive, political, or critical of Thai authorities. **All mail is screened by prison staff, so privacy is limited.** Include the inmate's full name, prison number, and the complete address of the facility to ensure proper delivery. While incoming letters are generally allowed, packages may be restricted or require prior approval. It's wise to contact the prison to confirm what can be sent.

Inmates in Thai prisons are **strictly prohibited from possessing or using cell phones.** Mobile phones are considered contraband, and being caught with one can result in severe disciplinary action for the inmate and legal penalties for anyone attempting to smuggle a device into the facility. However, inmates are allowed to make phone calls under controlled and supervised conditions, though they cannot receive incoming calls from outside. Phone calls must typically be requested in advance, and the numbers to be called often need to be pre-approved by prison authorities. These calls are conducted on monitored landlines within the facility, are usually time-limited, and may be supervised or recorded. The frequency and duration of phone access depend on the specific prison's policies, the inmate's behavior, and their legal status. While there is a general framework set by the Thai Department of Corrections, each prison has some discretion to set its own rules based on its security level and available resources. To receive a call from an inmate or to get added to their approved call list, it's best to contact the prison directly and inquire about their procedures.

Visiting an inmate in a Thai prison is allowed under **strict rules** that vary slightly between facilities. Typically, immediate family members—such as parents, spouses, children, and siblings—are permitted to visit, while friends or extended relatives may require prior approval. Some prisons require the inmate to register a list of approved visitors in advance. All visitors must present valid identification, such as a passport for foreigners or a Thai ID card for locals. Visits usually take place on weekdays during designated hours, with the frequency depending on the inmate's status. Those awaiting trial may receive more frequent visits, while convicted inmates are often limited to one or two visits per week. Visits are usually 15 to 30 minutes long and are often non-contact, conducted through a glass partition with communication via phone or intercom.

Before visiting, it's important to follow the prison's dress code—modest clothing is required, and items like shorts, sleeveless shirts, or revealing outfits are not permitted. Visitors should arrive early, as check-in and security screening can take time. Personal belongings, including phones, wallets, and bags, must be stored in lockers outside the visiting area. If you're bringing approved items such as food, supplies, or money, these must be submitted for inspection according to the prison's procedures. Because rules and hours can vary by facility and are subject to change, it's always best to contact the prison directly in advance to confirm their current policies and ensure a smooth visit.

Prison Scams

Scams related to prisoners in Thai prisons are unfortunately quite common, especially targeting the families and friends of foreign inmates. Scammers often exploit the emotional stress and urgency felt by loved ones by **impersonating lawyers, prison officials, or intermediaries** who promise to speed up legal processes, secure early release, or improve prison conditions in exchange for large fees. These promises are almost always fraudulent and designed to extort money without providing any real help. Sometimes, scammers claim there are urgent fines, bribes, or "special fees" that must be paid immediately to avoid worse penalties or transfer the inmate to a better facility—none of which are legitimate demands under Thai law.

Red flags to watch out for include unsolicited contact from unknown individuals claiming to represent the inmate or the prison, requests for immediate or unusually high payments through untraceable methods like cryptocurrency, wire transfers, or money transfer services, and vague or inconsistent information about the inmate's case or condition. Scammers may also pressure you to keep the transaction confidential or refuse to allow direct contact with the prisoner. They often discourage you from reaching out to official authorities or the embassy, and may use aggressive or emotional tactics to push for quick payments. Be especially cautious if the person claiming to help asks for payment upfront without any formal documentation, receipts, or legal agreements.

If you suspect you are being scammed, it is crucial to **cease communication immediately and report the situation to the prison authorities**, your country's embassy in Thailand, and local law enforcement. Embassies can help verify the legitimacy of claims and provide guidance on how to proceed. Consulting a reputable Thai lawyer is also highly recommended to help confirm the authenticity of any demands and to assist with legitimate legal representation. Always rely on official channels and verified contacts, and never share personal, financial, or sensitive information with anyone who has not been thoroughly vetted. Staying informed and cautious can protect you and your loved one from falling victim to these exploitative schemes.

Upon Release

When a foreigner is released from a Thai prison, there are several important rules and obligations to be aware of. Typically, after serving their sentence, foreign inmates are expected to follow certain legal procedures before they can leave the country. In many cases, the Thai authorities will require the individual to report to immigration or other relevant government offices. Sometimes, deportation is mandatory, especially if the crime involved serious offenses or violated visa conditions. The person may also face a ban on re-entering Thailand for a specific period, depending on the nature of the offense and the length of their sentence.

Additionally, foreigners released from prison may be subject to restrictions such as reporting regularly to immigration authorities, especially if they are on probation or parole. They might also be required to comply with certain conditions set by the court, which could include restrictions on travel within Thailand or limitations on certain activities. Failure to comply with these post-release obligations can lead to further legal trouble or re-arrest. It's important for anyone released from a Thai prison to consult with a lawyer or their embassy to fully understand their rights, obligations, and the proper procedures for reintegration or departure from the country.

THE ADMINISTRATION OF JUSTICE

CHAPTER 13

THE ADMINISTRATION
OF JUSTICE

Thailand's Legal System

Thailand's legal system is deeply influenced by its historical roots and the country's efforts to modernize while preserving national sovereignty. The historical foundation lies in a blend of Hindu-Brahmin laws and Theravada Buddhist principles, collectively known as *Dhammasattha*. These customary laws emphasized moral conduct, hierarchical social structures, and the king's role as a divine and righteous lawgiver. The country's first major legal reforms took place under King Chulalongkorn (Rama V) in the late 19th century, as Thailand sought to resist colonization by adopting Western-style institutions. During this period, legal codes were drafted with assistance from European advisors, especially drawing on civil law traditions from France and Germany.

The current Thai legal system is classified as a **civil law system**, relying heavily on codified statutes as opposed to judicial precedent. The most significant legal codes include the Civil and Commercial Code, the Criminal Code, and the Civil and Criminal Procedure Codes. Laws are drafted by the Council of State and enacted by the National Assembly. In this system, court rulings may hold persuasive value but do not establish binding precedent, unlike in common law jurisdictions.

Thailand's judiciary is composed of four main branches. The **Court of Justice** is the general court system that handles both civil and criminal cases. The **Administrative Court** is responsible for resolving disputes between individuals and government agencies, including cases involving alleged abuse of power. The **Constitutional Court** plays a pivotal role in interpreting the constitution, assessing the legality of laws, and settling high-profile political disputes. Finally, the **Military Court** handles matters involving military personnel and, during periods of emergency or military control, may also try civilians.

Distinctive features of Thailand's judiciary include the expansive powers of the Constitutional Court and the central role of the monarchy in legal legitimacy. Although judicial decisions are not binding in the way precedents are in common law systems, judgments by the Constitutional and Supreme Courts significantly influence how lower courts interpret statutes. The judiciary is intended to operate independently, but in practice, political dynamics and appointments often cast doubt on this independence.

Challenges to Thailand's legal system are numerous. A primary concern is the **frequent rewriting of the Constitution**—Thailand has had 20 different constitutions since 1932, largely as a result of repeated military coups. The 2017 Constitution, drafted under military rule, has been criticized for entrenching the military's influence in both legal and political institutions Additionally, **freedom of expression** is constrained by laws such as Article 112 of the Criminal Code (the *lèse-majesté* law), which criminalizes insults to the monarchy. This law has been used to suppress political dissent and limit public debate. Further issues include judicial delays, high legal costs, and limited access to justice for marginalized communities, all of which undermine public trust in the judiciary.

In summary, Thailand's legal system combines traditional moral principles with civil law structures imported from the West. While it features comprehensive codes and a diverse judiciary, its effectiveness is often challenged by political interference, constitutional instability, and human rights concerns. For the legal system to fulfill its democratic role, structural reforms aimed at judicial independence, legal accessibility, and human rights protections are critically needed.

General Questions

1. *Will the court treat first-time offenders and tourists with more leniency?* Thai courts may show some leniency toward first-time offenders and tourists, particularly in minor or non-violent cases, but this is not guaranteed and depends heavily on the circumstances of the offense and the judge's discretion. First-time offenders are often viewed more favorably if they show remorse, plead guilty, and have no prior criminal history. Tourists may also receive lighter penalties in less serious cases, especially if they cooperate with authorities and demonstrate respect for local laws. However, for serious crimes such as drug trafficking, violent offenses, or acts deemed offensive to the monarchy, the courts apply the law strictly regardless of whether the individual is a foreigner or has no prior convictions.

2. *If I am charged with a crime, which court is likely to hear my case?* If you are charged with a crime in Thailand, your case will most likely be heard by the **Court of Justice**, which handles both criminal and civil cases. Within this system, lower courts such as the **Provincial Court** or the **District Court** will usually be the first to hear your case, depending on the seriousness of the offense and where it occurred. More serious or complex cases may be escalated to the **Criminal Court** in Bangkok or eventually to the **Appeals** or **Supreme Court** if there are appeals. If the charge involves a government agency or official misconduct, the **Administrative Court** may become involved, while certain national security or emergency cases might be tried in a **Military Court**, especially if martial law is in effect.

3. *What is the standard of proof in a criminal case in Thailand?*
   The standard of proof in a criminal case in Thailand is "**beyond a reasonable doubt**," meaning the prosecution must present sufficient and convincing evidence to prove the defendant's guilt to such a degree that there is no reasonable doubt in the mind of the judge. If any reasonable doubt remains about the defendant's guilt, the court is required to acquit the accused. This standard is intended to protect the presumption of innocence, ensuring that no one is convicted unless the evidence clearly establishes their guilt.

Law of the Land True Story[18]

Paul Chambers, an American political scientist teaching in Thailand, was arrested in April 2025 for allegedly violating Thailand's lèse-majesté law (Article 112), which prohibits insulting the monarchy. The charges were related to his involvement in organizing an academic webinar held in Singapore that discussed Thailand's monarchy and political issues. Although Chambers did not create or publicly endorse the controversial content, Thai authorities held him responsible due to his role in the event.

The arrest drew widespread criticism from human rights groups and academic circles, who argued that it infringed on freedom of expression and academic freedom. The U.S. government also expressed concern, urging Thailand to respect international standards on free speech. The event sent a chilling message to activists, academics, journalists, and foreigners living in Thailand that discussing or criticizing the monarchy could lead to serious legal consequences. This reflects the broader use of Article 112 as a political tool to suppress dissent and limit public debate, often targeting those calling for reform or government accountability. Overall, the case illustrates how the lèse-majesté law restricts freedom of expression and is used to silence opposition.

---

18 https://www.washingtonpost.com/world/2025/04/09/thailand-us-academic-arrested-lese-majeste

 **Takeaways**

- Thailand's legal system blends traditional Hindu-Buddhist principles with Western civil law influences, emphasizing codified statutes rather than judicial precedent.

- The judiciary consists of the Court of Justice (civil/criminal), Administrative Court (government disputes), Constitutional Court (constitutional interpretation), and Military Court (military and some civilian cases under martial law).

- Political interference, frequent constitutional changes, and military influence affect the judiciary's independence and effectiveness.

- Laws like Article 112 (lèse-majesté) strictly criminalize insults to the monarchy, limiting freedom of expression and being used to suppress dissent.

- Judicial delays, high costs, and limited access for marginalized groups undermine public trust and highlight the need for legal reforms to improve fairness and rights protection.

CRIME VICTIM ASSISTANCE

CHAPTER 14
CRIME VICTIM ASSISTANCE

Overview

In Thailand, victims of crime have access to a variety of support through government programs and non-governmental organizations that provide legal, psychological, and practical assistance. The **Royal Thai Police**[19] are the first point of contact for victims, with special units such as the Women and Children Protection Centers established to address sensitive cases, including domestic violence, sexual assault, and human trafficking. The police cooperate closely with the **Ministry of Social Development and Human Security**[20], which oversees social welfare programs including victim protection, rehabilitation, and shelter services for vulnerable groups. For example, MSDHS operates emergency shelters and provides counseling services to victims of abuse and trafficking. The Ministry of Justice also plays an important role in victim support by facilitating access to legal aid through the **Office of the Judiciary**[21], which offers free or low-cost legal services to victims who cannot afford private representation. This helps victims participate effectively in the legal process and understand their rights. In cases involving human trafficking, the Department of Special Investigation provides specialized investigative support and victim protection programs.

---

19 www.royalthaipolice.go.th

20 www.m-society.go.th

21 www.coj.go.th

Non-governmental organizations (NGO's) complement government efforts by providing tailored services and advocacy. Organizations such as the **Thai Women's Crisis Center**[22] offer safe housing, counseling, and legal assistance primarily to women and children who have experienced violence or trafficking. The **Mirror Foundation**[23] is another NGO active in rescuing and rehabilitating trafficking victims and marginalized groups. These NGOs often work with international bodies like the United Nations and cooperate with government agencies to strengthen victim assistance frameworks. The **United Nations Office on Drugs and Crime in Thailand**[24] also supports anti-trafficking efforts and victim protection.

Emergency contact numbers are critical for immediate help. The general police emergency number is **191**, which connects callers to local police stations anywhere in Thailand. The Tourist Police can be reached at **1155** and are specially trained to assist foreign visitors in dealing with crime, language barriers, and safety issues. Victims of domestic violence and child abuse can call the Women and Children Protection Hotline at **1300** for confidential support and referral to shelters or counseling services. Medical emergencies are handled through the national ambulance service at **1669**. Human trafficking cases can be reported via the Anti-Trafficking Hotline **1171**, managed by the Ministry of Social Development and Human Security, which provides victim assistance and coordinates rescue operations.

These organizations and government offices provide critical support for victims navigating the legal system, accessing shelter, medical care, and psychological services. Despite this infrastructure, challenges remain in ensuring timely and equitable access, especially for marginalized groups and foreigners.

---

22   www.twcc.or.th

23   www.mirror.or.th

24   www.unodc.org

What to Do If You Are the Victim of a Crime

If you become the victim of a crime in Thailand, the first and most important step is to ensure your safety by moving away from any immediate danger. If you require urgent medical attention, you should call the ambulance service at **1669** or go to the nearest hospital as soon as possible. Once you are safe, it is essential to **report the crime** promptly by contacting the police. You can dial the emergency number **191** or visit the nearest police station to file a report. Additionally, the **Tourist Police**, reachable at **1155**, can provide assistance and help bridge any language barriers.

It is important to preserve any evidence related to the crime. Avoid disturbing the crime scene or washing off any physical evidence, and keep any relevant items such as messages, photos, or documents that might support the investigation. If you do not speak Thai, you should request an **interpreter** or bring someone who can translate to ensure clear communication with the authorities. Seeking **medical** and **psychological support** is also critical, even if your injuries seem minor. Getting a medical examination and keeping records of any treatment you receive can be valuable for your case. Counseling services are often available through hospitals and non-governmental organizations to help you cope with emotional trauma.

Understanding your **legal rights** as a victim is crucial. You have the right to access **legal assistance**, and the **Office of the Judiciary** offers free or low-cost legal aid to victims. You should also reach out to NGOs or government agencies specializing in victim support for services such as shelter, counseling, or rehabilitation. The Ministry of Social Development and Human Security runs victim protection programs and operates emergency shelters for those in need.

You should also **contact your country's embassy or consulate** as they can provide important assistance by referring you to trusted counseling services, medical professionals, and legal advisors who speak your language and understand your cultural background. While embassies do not offer counseling directly, they help facilitate communication with local authorities and connect you to mental health support and victim services. Consular officials can also provide emotional support, guide you through Thailand's legal and healthcare systems, assist with arranging legal representation, emergency travel documents, and coordinate with your family back home.

It is very important to keep copies of all **reports, medical records, and legal documents** related to your case. These documents serve as crucial evidence and help you keep track of every step in the legal process. For example, police reports detail the initial complaint and investigation, while medical records document any injuries or treatment, which can be vital for proving harm or the severity of the crime. Legal documents, including court summons, filings, and judgments, provide updates on the progress and status of your case.

Equally important is staying **informed** about your case by **regularly communicating** with the police, prosecutors, or your legal representatives. Following up helps prevent delays, clarifies any questions you may have, and ensures that your case receives the attention it deserves. Missing court hearings or failing to cooperate with investigators can negatively impact the outcome, so it is essential to attend all scheduled hearings and provide any requested information or testimony promptly. By being proactive and engaged, you not only support the legal process but also strengthen your position in seeking justice.

Common Tourist Scams in Thailand

Tourists in Thailand are sometimes targeted by various scams that can range from minor annoyances to costly traps. One frequent scam involves **tuk-tuk drivers or taxi drivers** who offer tours at unusually low prices but then take passengers to overpriced shops or charge extra fees. Another common trick is the **"gem scam,"** where tourists are persuaded to buy supposedly valuable gems at inflated prices, often under pressure from friendly strangers or touts. **Jet ski scams** at beach resorts are also notorious, where tourists are accused of damaging rented jet skis and asked to pay large fines without evidence.

In cities like Bangkok, scams involving **fake travel agents** or **ticket sellers** are widespread; they may sell counterfeit tickets for popular attractions or claim certain sites are closed to redirect tourists to other costly tours. Additionally, some scammers use the **"broken meter" tactic** in taxis, turning off the meter and demanding a fixed high fare. Another subtle scam involves **overcharging in restaurants or markets**, where tourists might be given inflated bills or shortchanged in change.

Be cautious if an offer seems too good to be true, such as unusually cheap tours or "special" deals from strangers. Always **use official taxi services or ride-hailing apps** like Grab, which have fixed pricing and help avoid meter-related disputes. For tuk-tuks, agree on the fare upfront and be wary of unsolicited offers to take you to shops. Avoid purchasing gems, jewelry, or souvenirs from vendors who pressure you or offer overly discounted prices.

When booking tours or tickets, **use reputable companies** or official counters rather than street vendors. Always **inspect rental equipment carefully** before use, take photos or videos, and get any agreements in writing to protect yourself against false damage claims. In markets and restaurants, **check your bills carefully**, and if possible, ask locals or hotel staff for recommendations on trustworthy places.

Trust your instincts—if someone is pushing too hard or the situation feels off, politely decline and walk away. Staying informed and vigilant can help you enjoy your trip without falling victim to these common scams.

Sexual Assault

If you are a victim of sexual assault in Thailand, the first and most important step is to get to a safe place and call for help. You can dial **191** to reach the local police for immediate assistance, or **1155** to contact the Tourist Police, who are trained to assist foreigners and can often speak English. If you are in need of emotional or emergency support, you can also call **1300**, a national hotline that offers confidential help for victims of violence, including sexual assault. Your embassy or consulate can also play a key role—they can provide guidance, help you find legal or medical support, and assist with communication and emergency arrangements.

As soon as you are safe, it is vital to seek **medical care**. Go directly to a hospital, preferably a major public hospital or a reputable private facility in the area. Hospitals such as **Police General Hospital** in Bangkok or large provincial hospitals are equipped to handle sexual assault cases and can conduct a forensic examination if requested. Let the medical staff know that you have been sexually assaulted and that you may file a police report. They will help preserve medical evidence, provide treatment for injuries, offer emergency contraception, and test for sexually transmitted infections. If you feel overwhelmed, ask for a hospital social worker or interpreter, especially if you are a foreign visitor.

Once you've received medical attention, **reporting the incident to the police** is the next important step. You can go to the nearest police station, and if you are a tourist, the Tourist Police can assist you with translation and coordination. When you arrive, clearly tell them that you wish to report a sexual assault. You have the right to be treated respectfully and to request a female officer or interpreter. If you feel uncomfortable at a local station, you may ask to have your case handled at a larger station or in a city where there are more specialized resources.

Non-governmental organizations (NGOs) in Thailand play a vital role in supporting government efforts by providing specialized services and advocacy for vulnerable populations. The **Thai Women's Crisis Center (TWCC)**[25] offers safe housing, counseling, and legal assistance, focusing primarily on women and children affected by domestic violence, sexual assault, and trafficking. Another key NGO is the **Mirror Foundation**[26], which works extensively in northern Thailand on human trafficking cases, migrant worker rights, and rehabilitation of marginalized groups. Both organizations frequently collaborate with government agencies and international partners. Additionally, the **United Nations Office on Drugs and Crime (UNODC) Regional Office for Southeast Asia and**

---

25 www.twcc.or.th

26 www.mirror.or.th

the Pacific, based in Bangkok[27], actively supports Thailand's anti-trafficking initiatives, providing training, technical assistance, and policy guidance. Together, these NGOs and international bodies reinforce the national framework for victim protection and long-term recovery.

? General Questions

1. *If I am a victim of a crime, can I legally be compensated?* **Yes.** If you are a victim of a crime in Thailand, you can legally receive compensation through the **Ministry of Justice's compensation scheme** under the Victim Compensation Act. This covers medical expenses, loss of income, psychological support, and, in serious cases, death or disability—recent updates in 2025 increased the maximum payouts (e.g., up to 80,000 THB ($ 2,150 USD) for medical care and 300,000 THB ($8,100 USD) for death or disability). To qualify, you must report the crime, receive medical care, and apply within one year via a provincial justice office. You may also seek restitution through a criminal trial under Section 44/1 of the Criminal Procedure Code, or file a separate civil lawsuit. New laws, such as the Anti-Torture and Enforced Disappearance Act, offer additional fixed compensation for specific human rights violations.

2. *If a family member falls victim to homicide, can I bring the body back to my home country?* **Yes.** If a family member is the victim of homicide in Thailand, you can bring their body back to your home country, but it involves several legal and logistical steps. Thai authorities require an autopsy for all unnatural deaths, which can delay the release of the body. After the investigation and issuance of a Thai death certificate, you'll need documents like an embalming certificate and a permit for international transport. Your embassy or consulate can assist with

---

27 www.unodc.org

coordinating local authorities, funeral services, and required paperwork. Repatriation can be expensive and may take days or weeks, depending on the case and official procedures.

3. *If a family member falls victim to homicide, will I receive any assistance from the Thai government?* **Yes.** If a family member is killed in Thailand, you may receive assistance from the Thai government through the Ministry of Justice's **Victim Compensation scheme** and the **Justice Fund.** These programs can provide financial support for funeral expenses, loss of family income, and emotional distress—typically up to 100,000 THB ($2,700 USD) or more, depending on circumstances. Applications are made through provincial justice offices, and you don't need to wait for a conviction to apply. If the death involves state wrongdoing or discrimination, additional support may be available through the **Rights and Liberties Protection Department** or the **National Human Rights Commission.** Legal aid and counseling are also offered, though the process can be complex and slow.

POLICE

CHAPTER 15
POLICE

Overview

Thailand's police system is entirely centralized under the **Royal Thai Police** (**RTP**), with no separate state or municipal forces. It operates through a hierarchy that includes regional commands and Bangkok's **Metropolitan Police Bureau**, as well as specialized units like the **Tourist Police**, **Immigration Bureau**, **Special Branch Bureau**, and **Border Patrol Police**, all under one national command structure. Leadership flows from the **Commissioner-General** (appointed in October 2024) through multiple deputies and assistant directors overseeing regional and functional bureaus.

The RTP employs around **210,000 to 230,000 officers**, making it one of the largest police forces globally by headcount—approximately 17% of Thailand's civilian government workforce.[28] Official crime data from 2024 shows that Thai police handled over 500,000 criminal cases and resolved about 93% of them, including serious criminal and cybercrime cases, indicating strong case-handling capacity.[29]

However, staffing adequacy remains an issue. Many police stations, particularly in suburban or rural provinces, operate with **personnel**

28 https://en.wikipedia.org/wiki/Royal_Thai_Police

29 https://www.khaosodenglish.com/news/2024/12/31/
    thai-police-solve-93-of-more-than-500000-cases-in-2024/

shortages. Financial pressures on officers are also significant, with accumulated debt among RTP personnel reaching nearly 300 billion THB. The national police chief has candidly addressed how these welfare and staffing issues may impact morale and service quality.[30]

Police Response

The Thai police system is composed of several specialized branches, each with distinct functions that contribute to national security, law enforcement, and public safety. The **Royal Thai Police**, which acts as the central authority overseeing all policing operations throughout the country. This central command coordinates national-level investigations, ensures law and order, and handles policy development and oversight. Within the Royal Thai Police structure, the **Metropolitan Police Bureau** is responsible for policing the capital, Bangkok, where it manages urban crime, traffic control, and public demonstrations. Due to Bangkok's political significance, this bureau often plays a critical role in crowd control during protests and high-profile political events.

Outside of Bangkok, the country is divided into multiple **provincial police regions**, each responsible for a specific geographic area. These regional forces manage everything from petty crime to serious criminal investigations, while also addressing local issues such as domestic violence, drug trafficking, and rural security. The **Central Investigation Bureau**, a specialized unit within the Royal Thai Police, handles more complex criminal cases, including organized crime, financial fraud, cybercrime, and other serious offenses that often require national or international coordination.

Another important branch is the **Tourist Police**, which focuses on safeguarding foreign visitors and supporting tourism-related security. Officers in this unit are typically multilingual and trained to assist tourists who encounter legal or safety issues. The **Narcotics Suppression Bureau** is dedicated to dismantling drug trafficking networks and works

---

30 https://thethaiger.com/news/national/
thai-police-officers-face-bankruptcy-with-debt-over-300-billion-baht

closely with both domestic and international partners to tackle the drug trade. Its work often includes undercover operations and large-scale raids, especially in border regions. Meanwhile, the **Immigration Bureau** enforces visa regulations and monitors illegal immigration, working to detect human trafficking and cross-border crime.

Despite this organizational structure and specialization, the Thai police face a number of persistent and complex challenges. One of the most significant issues is **widespread public perception of corruption** within the force. Incidents involving bribery, abuse of power, and lack of transparency have deeply eroded public trust over the years. **Political interference** is another major concern, with the police often accused of acting on behalf of powerful political interests, especially during periods of unrest or when handling sensitive political cases. This has led to perceptions of unequal enforcement of the law.

In addition to internal challenges, the force also struggles with **resource disparities**. While urban areas like Bangkok may have relatively well-equipped units, many rural police stations operate with limited budgets, outdated equipment, and insufficient personnel. Training standards also vary, and there is a growing need for improved education in areas such as digital forensics, human rights, and international criminal law. The modernization of police work has not progressed evenly across the country, leaving some units unprepared for emerging threats such as cybercrime and transnational criminal networks.

Police and Community Relations

The overall image of the Thai police—both within Thailand and on the international stage—is mixed, leaning toward negative in key areas, particularly regarding public trust, transparency, and professionalism.

Domestically, the perception of the Thai police is often shaped by widespread concerns about corruption, political bias, and lack of accountability. Many Thai citizens see the police as deeply intertwined with the political elite, often serving the interests of those in power rather than upholding justice impartially. This perception has been reinforced by repeated incidents involving bribery, abuse of authority, and selective law enforcement, especially during political protests or high-profile criminal investigations. Traffic police, in particular, are frequently cited in public complaints about extortion and "on-the-spot" fines. Although there are dedicated officers and professional units, these positive examples are often overshadowed by a broader sense that the institution as a whole lacks integrity and internal reform. Additionally, the public views the Thai police as overly hierarchical and resistant to change. Recruitment, promotion, and appointments within the force are often influenced more by connections and patronage than by merit or performance. This has resulted in a bureaucratic culture that many feel discourages transparency and accountability. Efforts at reform have been slow-moving, and despite promises from successive governments to clean up the force, progress has been limited and inconsistent.

Internationally, Thailand's police are generally seen as effective in certain areas—such as tourism security, major event management, and regional cooperation on transnational crime—but these successes are frequently undercut by concerns similar to those expressed at home. Human rights organizations have criticized Thai police for their handling of political dissent, use of force, and lack of judicial oversight. Cases of mistreatment of suspects, wrongful arrests, or coerced confessions have drawn international scrutiny, especially when foreign nationals are involved.

Moreover, foreign embassies and international agencies working in Thailand often maintain a cautious relationship with the police, recognizing both their essential role in law enforcement and the institutional weaknesses that limit their credibility. There have been successful collaborations in areas like anti-narcotics operations, counter-trafficking, and disaster response, but these tend to be led by specific, well-trained units rather than reflective of the police force as a whole.

Police Use of Force

Police use of force remains a **significant issue** in Thailand, with ongoing concerns both from the public and international human rights organizations. While Thai law allows police to use force when necessary—such as in self-defense or to maintain public order—there are frequent allegations that this force is used disproportionately, without sufficient oversight, and sometimes in violation of human rights.

Over the past few years, several high-profile incidents have drawn national and international criticism. One of the most notorious recent cases was in 2021, involving the death of a drug suspect in Nakhon Sawan Province (see Law of the Land True Story below). The case severely damaged public trust and highlighted systemic issues around impunity and abuse of power.

Beyond this, during the pro-democracy protests in 2020–2021, numerous reports emerged of police using excessive force to disperse crowds, including rubber bullets, tear gas, and water cannons. Protesters, including minors, were sometimes injured, and human rights groups criticized the disproportionate response to largely peaceful demonstrations. These events brought Thailand under scrutiny from organizations such as Amnesty International and Human Rights Watch, which documented patterns of violent crackdowns and arbitrary detentions.

Moreover, in many rural or remote areas, less-publicized cases continue to surface involving beatings during arrest, deaths in custody, or torture during interrogations. Often, these cases are under-investigated or dismissed, leading to perceptions that police officers enjoy a high degree of immunity from prosecution.

 **Law of the Land True Story**[31]

In August 2021, in Nakhon Sawan Province, a drug suspect died during a brutal interrogation at the hands of Pol. Col. Thitisan Utthanaphon, the local police chief, and several officers. The suspect and his girlfriend

---

31   https://www.theguardian.com/world/2021/aug/26/
     thai-police-chief-accused-of-killing-suspect-in-custody-is-arrested

had been arrested for drug possession. During questioning, Thitisan allegedly tried to extort 2 million baht (about $55,000 USD) from the man. When the suspect couldn't pay, officers suffocated him by placing multiple plastic bags over his head, as seen in leaked CCTV footage from inside the station.

The police claimed he died of a drug overdose, but the video, leaked by a junior officer, showed the suspect being slowly suffocated while Thitisan watched and gave orders. The footage caused national outrage. Thitisan, known as "Jo Ferrari" for his fleet of luxury cars allegedly seized during police operations, fled but later surrendered.

He and six others were arrested and tried. In 2022, Thitisan was convicted of murder. His initial death sentence was later commuted to life imprisonment. The case shocked the nation and exposed deep-rooted problems of corruption, abuse of power, and lack of accountability in the Thai police. While the conviction was seen as a rare act of justice, public distrust in law enforcement remains high.

CHAPTER 16

HOW TO GET LEGAL HELP IN THAILAND

HOW TO GET LEGAL HELP IN THAILAND

Available Resources

If you're arrested in Thailand, the first thing you should do is **contact your country's embassy or consulate.** While they can't get you out of jail, they can ensure you're being treated fairly, provide a list of local lawyers, notify your family if needed, and assist with communication in your language.

You'll likely be taken to a local police station where you can ask to contact your embassy and request legal representation. Always remain calm and avoid signing anything you don't understand, especially if it's in Thai.

To find reliable legal representation, embassies typically keep a list of trustworthy, English-speaking law firms in Thailand. Well-known international or regional law firms like **Tilleke & Gibbins, Siam Legal**, and **Baker McKenzie** (Thailand office) are often recommended. You can also check with the Thai Bar Association, known as the **Lawyer Council of Thailand** for licensed lawyers.

There are also **non-profit organizations** that offer legal help to visitors in specific situations. The **International Justice Mission (IJM)** may assist in cases involving abuse, exploitation, or human trafficking. The **Human Rights and Development Foundation (HRDF)** helps migrants and vulnerable individuals navigate legal issues. **Thai Lawyers for Human Rights (TLHR)** supports people involved in political or human rights-related cases. For asylum seekers, the **UNHCR** Thailand office may also provide legal and humanitarian assistance.

If you are detained, ask for an interpreter, call your embassy, and avoid signing documents unless you're sure what they say. Having emergency numbers saved and written down in advance is always a good idea, especially when traveling abroad.

U.S. Embassy – Bangkok

95 Wireless Road, Bangkok 10330
+66 2 205 4049 (during office hours)
+66 2 205 4000 (after hours / emergencies)
From the U.S.: +1 202 640 2632
Email: acsbkk@state.gov

U.S. Consulate – Chiang Mai

387 Witchayanond Road, Chiang Mai 50300
+66 53 107 777 (during office hours)
+66 81 881 1878 (after hours)
Email: acschn@state.gov

Other Important Contacts

Thai Police: 191
Tourist Police (English-speaking): 1155
Social Help Centre (for vulnerable persons): 1300
Lawyers Council of Thailand: www.lawyerscouncil.or.th

Legal Aid

Foreign visitors in Thailand may be eligible for legal aid, though the system is primarily designed for Thai nationals. Eligibility depends on the nature of the case and the applicant's financial situation. Legal aid is more likely to be granted in criminal cases, especially if the individual cannot afford legal representation and faces serious charges such as detention or trial. Foreigners involved in cases related to human rights, immigration detention, trafficking, or labor exploitation may also receive assistance, particularly from non-governmental organizations.

The process typically begins by contacting the **Legal Aid Centre** at the Lawyers Council of Thailand. Applications can be made at their office or through legal aid desks found in some provincial courts. You will need to present your passport, visa status, and basic case details. Embassies can also help facilitate contact with legal aid providers and may offer guidance on how to apply. In certain cases, NGOs such as the Human Rights and Development Foundation (HRDF) or Thai Lawyers for Human Rights (TLHR) may step in to provide free legal assistance or refer you to lawyers willing to take your case pro bono.

To qualify for legal aid, you usually must demonstrate financial hardship and that the case involves serious consequences such as risk to liberty or fundamental rights. Aid is generally not available for minor civil disputes, visa overstays, or non-criminal matters unless tied to a larger human rights issue.

Legal aid in Thailand can cover legal consultation, court representation, interpreter services, and help with legal documentation or appeals. While the resources for foreigners are more limited than for Thai citizens, assistance is possible—especially if the case involves detention, rights violations, or criminal prosecution.

Foreign Embassies in Thailand

Thailand's capital, Bangkok, is home to most of the country's foreign embassies, hosting **nearly 80 resident diplomatic missions** from prominent countries such as the United States, China, Japan, Germany, the United Kingdom, France, Australia, and India. Besides **Bangkok**, key cities like **Chiang Mai**, **Phuket**, and **Pattaya** have consulates or honorary consulates to assist foreigners in those regions. These diplomatic missions provide vital services including assistance to their citizens who face legal troubles, emergencies, or need consular support such as passport renewals and travel advisories.

Foreign embassies and consulates in Thailand are respected and protected under international law, particularly the **Vienna Convention on Diplomatic Relations**. This grants them diplomatic immunity, ensuring their premises, staff, and communications are safeguarded from interference by Thai authorities. This protection allows them to perform their duties independently and securely, offering consular services, protecting their citizens abroad, and facilitating diplomatic communication.

In practice, these missions play a crucial role in assisting foreign nationals during emergencies like arrests or medical crises. Thai authorities generally cooperate with foreign missions, permitting embassy staff to visit detained nationals, provide lists of local lawyers, and help ensure their rights under Thai law are respected. However, embassies cannot interfere with local judicial processes or secure release from detention.

Foreign missions also contribute to cultural exchange, trade promotion, and political dialogue, strengthening bilateral ties. Some countries maintain honorary consuls in provincial areas to provide limited consular assistance outside Bangkok. Despite occasional diplomatic sensitivities, foreign embassies in Thailand are treated with professionalism and respect, reflecting Thailand's commitment to international norms and its role as a major regional hub.

MEDICAL FACILITIES & HOSPITALS

MEDICAL FACILITIES & HOSPITALS

Overview

Thailand's healthcare system is generally regarded as **one of the best in Southeast Asia**, offering a mix of public and private services. The country has made significant investments in healthcare infrastructure, resulting in modern hospitals and clinics, especially in urban areas like Bangkok, Chiang Mai, and Phuket. Public hospitals provide affordable care and are supported by the **Universal Health Coverage scheme**, which covers Thai nationals and some permanent residents, but foreigners typically pay out of pocket or use private insurance.

Healthcare operates through a **tiered system**, with primary care available at community health centers and more specialized services offered at district, provincial, and regional hospitals. Private hospitals tend to provide higher-quality facilities and services, often staffed by English-speaking doctors, but their fees are higher than public hospitals.

Medical services in Thailand are generally accessible in cities and popular tourist destinations, with many facilities accredited internationally for quality and safety. Rural areas may have limited access to advanced care, but basic medical services are usually available. Affordability varies widely; public hospitals are low cost but may have longer wait times, while private care is more expensive but offers faster, more comfortable treatment.

Visitors' Access to Healthcare in Thailand

Visitors to Thailand can access medical services relatively easily, especially in cities and popular tourist destinations. Most foreigners pay for treatment through **travel insurance, private international health insurance,** or **out-of-pocket.** Public hospitals will treat foreigners but generally require immediate payment. Private hospitals often expect proof of insurance or a deposit before treatment begins. These private facilities are typically preferred by visitors for their speed, modern equipment, and English-speaking staff.

Private and travel insurance play a major role in accessing care. Short-term visitors are encouraged to purchase comprehensive travel insurance before arriving in Thailand. These policies often cover emergency medical treatment, hospital stays, outpatient care, and in some cases, medical evacuation or repatriation. Many plans also include coverage for trip cancellations, lost baggage, and personal liability. However, travelers should carefully check that their policy covers common activities in Thailand, such as motorbike riding or diving, as these are sometimes excluded. Longer-term visitors, expats, or digital nomads often purchase international health insurance or Thai-based plans from providers such as **Bupa Thailand, Pacific Cross, Luma, Aetna,** or **AXA.** These plans generally provide broader coverage and may offer direct billing arrangements with hospitals, meaning less need to pay up front and file claims later.

Most major private hospitals in Thailand—like Bumrungrad International, Bangkok Hospital, and Samitivej—have international patient centers that assist with insurance claims and can often process policies from well-known global providers. However, depending on the insurer and policy, patients may still need to pay first and seek reimbursement. It's recommended that travelers carry both printed and digital copies of their insurance policy and emergency contacts and clarify the claims process before travel.

Language barriers in healthcare can vary. In private hospitals, especially in urban areas, many medical staff speak English and are experienced with international patients. In contrast, public hospitals and smaller clinics may have limited English-speaking staff, which can create challenges. Interpreter services are not always available, so using a translation app or carrying a medical history translated into Thai can be helpful.

Thailand is also a hub for **medical tourism**, known for affordable, high-quality dental work, cosmetic procedures, and wellness treatments. While these services are professionally delivered, visitors should always check the credentials of clinics and practitioners. Visitors should be aware that **upfront payment is generally required**, even in emergencies. Having proper insurance is not just recommended—it's essential. It provides access to faster, higher-quality care and protects against potentially high medical costs. Without coverage, even minor hospital visits can become financially burdensome.

For **non-emergency medical needs** in Thailand—such as minor illnesses, prescription refills, or access to common medications—visitors will find the healthcare system very accessible, particularly in urban and tourist areas.

Thailand has a **vast network of pharmacies**, many of which are well-stocked and staffed by licensed pharmacists who can provide basic consultations. Medications that require a prescription in other countries—such as antibiotics, antihistamines, birth control pills, and even some blood pressure or cholesterol medications—can often be **purchased over the counter** in Thailand. However, regulations are tightening in urban areas, so some drugs may now require a valid prescription, especially controlled medications like opioids or psychiatric drugs.

If a visitor needs a **prescription refill** for medication brought from home, they can usually get one by visiting a **general practitioner or local clinic**, especially in tourist hubs like Bangkok, Phuket, and Chiang Mai. These visits are quick and affordable, with private clinics charging modest fees. Larger hospitals also have outpatient departments where walk-in patients can consult doctors for routine issues or refills. For travelers with chronic conditions, it's a good idea to bring a **copy of your prescription** and a doctor's note explaining your diagnosis and dosage, ideally translated into English or Thai. This makes it easier to obtain a local prescription if needed.

Visitors should also note that travel insurance typically does not cover non-emergency visits or regular medication unless explicitly stated, so expect to pay out of pocket for routine care or refills. Fortunately, costs are generally low compared to Western countries.

Hospitals in Thailand

Thailand has a **well-established and growing healthcare system**, with sources reporting around **1,300 hospitals nationwide**, including both public and private facilities. The public sector dominates in terms of numbers, with over **900 government-run hospitals**, while the private sector operates more than **400 hospitals**, many of which cater to both local and international patients.[32] As of 2023, Thailand had an estimated doctor-to-population ratio of approximately one doctor per 1,500 people, translating to around 67,000 physicians nationwide. This figure reflects steady improvements over the past decade, especially since 2014, as the country has expanded its healthcare workforce to meet rising demand. Compared to the global average of 17 doctors per 10,000 population reported by the World Health Organization in 2022, Thailand still lags slightly, but continues to make progress.

While infrastructure development has continued, Thailand's ratio of hospital beds remains relatively modest, particularly rural areas. However, despite some resource limitations, Thailand is widely recognized for the expertise of its medical professionals. The country is home to highly trained specialists in fields such as cardiology, orthopedics, oncology, and cosmetic surgery, many of whom have received international training or certifications. This specialized capacity has contributed to the country's reputation as a regional hub for both general healthcare and medical tourism.

Hospitals are most heavily concentrated in **urban centers**, particularly **Bangkok**, which serves as the medical hub of Thailand. Other cities with strong healthcare infrastructure include **Chiang Mai, Phuket, Pattaya,**

---

32 https://www.expatica.com/th/health/primary-care/
    thailand-hospital-2172910/

and **Khon Kaen**. In these locations, both public and private hospitals offer a wide range of services, including emergency care, outpatient clinics, and specialist treatment.

Thailand is internationally recognized for its **world-class private hospitals**, many of which cater specifically to foreigners and medical tourists. Some of the most well-known and highly rated hospitals include **Bumrungrad International Hospital** in Bangkok, one of the top international hospitals in Asia; **Bangkok Hospital**, which has a network across the country; **Samitivej Hospital**, known for its pediatrics and expat-friendly services; and **BNH Hospital**, which focuses on international patients and English-language care. These facilities are equipped with advanced technology, internationally trained doctors, and multilingual support staff. **Bangpakok International Hospital** markets itself as "The American Hospital of Bangkok," though it is not affiliated with the U.S. government. It offers American-standard care and English-speaking staff, and is part of a broader effort to attract international patients. Additionally, **Bumrungrad International** is often referred to as the "Mayo Clinic of Asia" and is popular with American, European, and Middle Eastern patients.

Public hospitals such as **Siriraj Hospital**, **Ramathibodi Hospital**, and **Chulalongkorn Memorial Hospital** in Bangkok are also respected, particularly for academic research, specialist services, and affordability. However, public hospitals often have longer wait times and fewer English-speaking staff compared to private institutions.

For international visitors seeking medical care, Thailand's private hospitals are generally the best option. They offer walk-in appointments, short wait times, international insurance handling, and high standards of care. Many even have **international departments** specifically designed to assist foreign patients with translation, insurance coordination, and travel support.

Overall, Thailand's hospital system provides excellent medical services, especially in private institutions that cater to global standards, making the country a major destination for both emergency and elective healthcare among international visitors.

General Questions

1. *What should you do if you feel unwell/sick in Thailand?* If you feel unwell or sick in Thailand, the first step is to assess the severity of your symptoms. For minor issues like a cold, stomach discomfort, or mild fever, you can visit a local pharmacy, which is often the quickest and most convenient option. Pharmacists in Thailand are knowledgeable and can recommend over-the-counter medication or refer you to a clinic if needed.

   If your symptoms are more serious or persistent, visit a nearby clinic or hospital. In tourist areas and cities, private clinics and hospitals are widely available, often with English-speaking staff. You can walk in without an appointment at most facilities. Bring your passport, insurance information (if you have coverage), and any medical history or medication list you may need.

   In case of a medical emergency—such as chest pain, difficulty breathing, high fever, or injury—call the national emergency medical services at **1669** for an ambulance. You can also go directly to the emergency department of the nearest hospital, where care is available 24/7.

   If you're unsure where to go, your hotel staff, embassy, or travel insurer's assistance hotline can help direct you to appropriate medical care.

2. *Are there any specialized medical facilities in Thailand for travelers who need urgent care or evacuation services?* Yes. Thailand offers specialized medical facilities and emergency services tailored for travelers who require urgent care or medical evacuation. In major cities like Bangkok, Chiang Mai, Phuket, and Pattaya, leading private hospitals such as Bumrungrad International Hospital, Bangkok Hospital, Samitivej Sukhumvit Hospital, and BNH Hospital are equipped to handle serious medical situations. These hospitals feature 24/7 emergency departments, intensive care units, and international departments

with multilingual staff. They are experienced in treating foreign patients and often assist with insurance claims, direct billing, and coordination with embassies or travel assistance providers.

For more critical or complex cases, Thailand also provides access to medical evacuation and air ambulance services through partnerships with global providers like International SOS, MedAire, and Falck Global Assistance. These services can arrange transport within Thailand or evacuation to a traveler's home country if necessary, depending on medical needs and insurance coverage. Since medical evacuation can be extremely costly, travelers are strongly advised to have comprehensive travel insurance that includes emergency evacuation benefits and to carry their insurance details and emergency contacts at all times while in the country.

Insurance Guidance

Foreign insurance plans are generally accepted at most major private hospitals in Thailand, especially those catering to international patients such as Bumrungrad International, Bangkok Hospital, and Samitivej. These hospitals often have dedicated insurance liaison offices that help process claims and coordinate with a wide range of global insurers. However, acceptance depends on the specific insurance provider and policy, so it's important to confirm coverage and whether the hospital has a direct billing agreement with your insurer before seeking treatment.

Medical costs in Thailand can vary significantly depending on the facility and type of care. A visit to a private hospital emergency room may cost anywhere from 2,000 to 10,000 THB (approximately $60 to $300 USD) or more, depending on the severity of the condition and tests required. A standard doctor's consultation typically ranges from 500 to 1,500 THB ($15 to $45 USD). Public hospitals are much more affordable but may involve longer waiting times and limited English support.

As mentioned before, payment is usually required upfront, especially at private facilities. Patients are often asked to provide a deposit or settle the bill before receiving non-emergency care. If your insurance provider has a direct billing arrangement with the hospital, you may only need to pay any deductible or non-covered expenses out of pocket. Otherwise, you may need to pay the full cost initially and submit a claim to your insurer for reimbursement later. It's advisable to carry both cash and credit cards, and to keep all medical and payment receipts for insurance claims.

CHAPTER 18
DRIVING IN THAILAND

IN THIS CHAPTER

- Overview
- Main Traffic Rules & Road Safety Tips
- General Questions
- Law of the Land Hypothetical

CHAPTER 18

DRIVING IN THAILAND

Overview

Driving in Thailand can be both an exciting and challenging experience, especially for foreign visitors unfamiliar with local traffic patterns and road customs. The overall driving environment varies widely depending on the region. In major cities like Bangkok, traffic congestion is common and can be intense, with frequent motorbikes weaving between cars. Outside urban areas, roads are generally less crowded but can be narrower and winding, especially in rural or mountainous regions. Drivers should remain alert and cautious, as driving styles can be aggressive compared to Western standards, and traffic rules are not always strictly followed.

The road infrastructure in Thailand is **relatively well-developed**, particularly on main highways and around urban centers. Expressways and highways connecting major cities are generally in good condition, with clear signage in both Thai and English. However, smaller rural roads may be less maintained, with potholes or uneven surfaces. Street lighting can be limited in some areas, so nighttime driving requires extra caution.

Foreign drivers must carry a **valid driver's license** from their home country along with an **International Driving Permit (IDP)** recognized in Thailand. An IDP is essential to avoid fines or legal issues, as Thai authorities may not accept foreign licenses alone. Vehicle insurance is mandatory, and foreign drivers should ensure they have at least third-party liability coverage. Rental car companies typically provide insurance options, but it's important to check the details and coverage limits carefully.

Drivers should be aware of some **local customs and signals** that may differ from their home countries. For example, using the horn is very common and is often used as a warning rather than an expression of frustration. Headlight flashing can signal intention to overtake or alert other drivers. Roundabouts are becoming more common but may not always be used correctly by other drivers. Lane discipline can be loose, and motorcycles frequently share lanes with cars. Seat belts are mandatory for front-seat passengers but less commonly used in the back seats.

Thailand has a network of **toll roads**, especially around Bangkok and on major highways such as the Motorway 7 and Expressway 9. Toll booths typically accept cash in Thai baht, and some also accept electronic payment cards or contactless systems like the **Easy Pass** or **M-Pass**. Foreign visitors renting cars can often obtain a toll pass from the rental company, allowing for convenient automatic payment. It's advisable to carry some cash when using toll roads, as not all booths accept cards or foreign currency.

Main Traffic Rules & Road Safety Tips

- **Driving Side:** In Thailand, vehicles drive on the **left side** of the road.
- **Speed Limits:** Speed limits typically range from **60 to 80 km/h (37 to 50 mph)** in urban areas and can go up to **120 km/h (75 mph)** on highways and expressways. Always watch for posted signs as limits can vary.
- **Traffic Signals:** Traffic lights use the standard red, yellow, and green system. However, not all drivers strictly obey signals, so caution is advised, especially at busy intersections.

- **Seat Belts:** Seat belts are **mandatory** for drivers and front-seat passengers. While not legally required for rear passengers, wearing them is strongly recommended for safety.

- **Alcohol:** The legal blood alcohol concentration (BAC) limit is **0.05%**. Enforcement is strict, and penalties for driving under the influence can include heavy fines, license suspension, or imprisonment.

- **Mobile Devices:** Using a mobile phone while driving is **illegal** unless using a hands-free system. Violations may result in fines or other penalties.

- **Toll Roads:** Toll roads are common on major highways and expressways. Payment is usually accepted in cash (Thai baht) and via electronic toll cards like Easy Pass or M-Pass. Rental cars often come with electronic toll passes for convenience.

- **If Stopped by Police:** Stay calm and polite. Present your driver's license, International Driving Permit, vehicle registration, and insurance documents. Fines are often payable on the spot, but if you choose to do so, always ask for an official receipt.

- **Road Safety:** Thailand's roads can be challenging due to heavy traffic, aggressive driving, and mixed road users. Awareness and caution are key to staying safe, especially for foreign drivers unfamiliar with local driving customs.

 ## General Questions

1. *Can I use my driver's license from my home country to drive Thailand?* **Yes.** You can use your home country driver's license to drive in Thailand only if it is accompanied by an International Driving Permit (IDP) recognized in Thailand. Without an IDP, your foreign license may not be legally accepted, and you could face fines or legal issues if stopped by police. It's important to carry both your original license and the IDP while driving. Some

countries have specific agreements with Thailand that may allow use of the home license alone, but generally, the IDP is required for foreign drivers.

2. *What is the age requirement for renting a car in Thailand?*
In Thailand, the minimum age to rent a car is usually 21, though some rental companies require drivers to be 23 or 25, especially for higher-end vehicles. Most companies also require that you've held a valid driver's license for at least one year, and if your license is not in English or Thai, an International Driving Permit (IDP) is typically required. Drivers under 25 may face a young driver surcharge, and some agencies may impose a maximum age limit around 70. Always check the specific rental company's terms in advance.

 **Law of the Land Hypothetical**

HYPOTHETICAL: *Emma rents a scooter in Phuket to explore the beaches. She wears a helmet, but her passenger chooses not to wear one for a short ride. They are soon stopped by Thai police at a checkpoint. Is it legally required for passengers on motorcycles or scooters to wear helmets in Thailand?*

ANSWER: *Yes. Under Thai law, both the driver and any passenger on a motorcycle or scooter are **legally required to wear helmets** at all times. Failure to do so can result in on-the-spot fines, regardless of the distance or location of the ride. While the driver may be wearing a helmet, the passenger's non-compliance makes both parties subject to penalties. Tourists are expected to follow the same traffic laws as locals, and police regularly enforce helmet regulations, particularly in areas popular with visitors.*

NUDE BEACHES & CLOTHING-OPTIONAL RESORTS

IN THIS CHAPTER

- Overview
- Legality and Safety
- General Questions
- Law of the Land True Story

NUDE BEACHES & CLOTHING-OPTIONAL RESORTS

Overview

Nudism is **generally not culturally acceptable** in Thailand and is generally frowned upon in public settings. Thai culture is conservative when it comes to modesty, and public nudity is considered inappropriate and can even lead to legal consequences under laws related to public indecency. Topless sunbathing or nude swimming, even in tourist-heavy areas, may result in fines or unwanted attention, as it contradicts social norms and local customs.

That said, there are a small number of private, clothing-optional resorts that discreetly cater to nudists, mostly targeting international visitors. These establishments are rare and operate with strict privacy policies, often located in remote or gated areas. Such places include niche naturist resorts in Pattaya, Phuket, or Chiang Mai, where nudism is allowed within the resort grounds but not outside them. These locations emphasize respect for Thai laws and cultural sensitivity, making clear that nudity is confined to private areas only. Public beaches, parks, and shared hotel spaces remain subject to standard decency laws, and nudity in these areas is not tolerated.

Legality and Safety

In Thailand, nudism is regulated through laws related to public decency and modesty, which are taken seriously under the country's legal and cultural framework, specifically **Section 388 of the Thai Penal Code**, which prohibits acts of public indecency. The standard penalty is a **fine of up to 500 THB, (approximately $15 USD)**. However, the situation can escalate depending on the setting and how authorities interpret the intent—particularly in religious sites, family areas, or places where locals file complaints.

If the act is deemed more serious—disruptive, offensive, or culturally insensitive—police may detain the individual, impose a larger fine unofficially, or refer the matter to immigration authorities. This can result in **visa cancellation, deportation**, or even **blacklisting** from future entry into Thailand.

If images or videos of the nude behavior are posted or shared online, charges may also fall under Thailand's **Computer Crimes Act**, which prohibits distribution of obscene material online. Penalties under this law can include **fines up to 100,000 THB (approximately $2,750–2,800 USD) and imprisonment for up to 10 years.**

In all cases, public nudity is not only illegal in Thailand but also regarded as deeply disrespectful to Thai cultural norms. Tourists are strongly advised to avoid any public nudity or semi-nude behavior outside of designated, private resorts where such activity is clearly permitted.

General Questions

1. *Is it allowed for tourists to sunbathe topless on a quiet or secluded beach in Thailand?* **No.** Even on a quiet or seemingly private beach, topless sunbathing is **not allowed** under Thai law. Public nudity, including going topless, is considered a form of public indecency regardless of how secluded the location might be. Thai cultural norms emphasize modesty, and such behavior is viewed as disrespectful. Local authorities may act on their own or in response to a complaint, and enforcement can occur without warning. Tourists are advised to avoid any form of public nudity outside designated private naturist resorts.

2. *Are there any private resorts in Thailand where nudism is allowed, and is it legal to be nude in such places?* **Yes.** There are a few private, clothing-optional resorts in Thailand where nudism is permitted within the confines of the property. These resorts cater specifically to naturists and operate discreetly in accordance with Thai law, which allows nudity on private property as long as it is not visible to the public and does not violate public decency statutes. Examples include **Oriental Village Chiang Mai, Barefeet Naturist Resort Bangkok,** and **Chan Resort Pattaya**— all of which are members of the **Naturist Association Thailand** (https://thailandnaturist.com), an organization that promotes respectful naturism in controlled environments. These resorts emphasize privacy, consent, and cultural sensitivity, and they often have strict rules to ensure that guests behave respectfully and within legal limits. While nudism is legal in these spaces, being nude outside the property (even briefly) can result in fines or legal action.

 **Law of the Land True Story** [33]

In April 2025, a Polish couple, 27-year-old man and 24-year-old woman, were arrested on Koh Phangan for public nudity after being seen embracing naked in the middle of Ban Tai Road and later sunbathing nude on Ban Kai Beach. Local residents alerted authorities, leading to their detention by police. The couple explained that they had undressed to express their love for each other. Both underwent drug tests, which returned negative results. The woman admitted to the offense and paid a 5,000 baht ($135 USD) fine before being released. The man, however, did not confess and was taken to the police station for further questioning. Authorities also requested the revocation of their tourist visas, leading to their deportation from Thailand .

This incident highlights Thailand's strict enforcement of public decency laws, which prohibit nudity in public spaces. Despite the couple's claim of expressing love, their actions were deemed a violation of Thai cultural norms and legal standards, resulting in legal consequences.

---

33 https://www.bangkokpost.com/thailand/general/3013947/
polish-couple-busted-for-nudity-on-koh-phangan

UNUSUAL LAWS

UNUSUAL LAWS

Overview

Unusual laws can be fascinating glimpses into a culture's values and history. While most people are aware of common legal restrictions, it's often the strange and quirky laws that capture our attention. These regulations can range from the amusing to the absurd, reflecting the unique circumstances and traditions of a place. Whether they arise from historical events, societal norms, or simply peculiar local customs, unusual laws can provide insight into the quirks of human behavior and governance.

 **Unusual Thai Laws and Associated Penalties**

Thailand has a number of unique laws that reflect its cultural values, social norms, and efforts to maintain public order. While some of these regulations may seem unusual or surprising to visitors, understanding and respecting them is important to avoid legal trouble during your stay. Beyond the well-known rules about respecting the monarchy and public decency, there are various other laws related to public behavior, health, and cultural sensitivities that travelers should be aware of. Here are some examples of such laws and the penalties associated with them:

- **Stepping On Thai Currency:** Because the currency bears the image of the King, stepping on money is seen as a serious sign of disrespect and can lead to **fines or arrest**.

- **Lèse-Majesté Law (Article 112):** Criticizing or insulting the monarchy is a severe offense in Thailand, punishable by **up to 15 years in prison**.

- **Chewing Gum Ban:** Chewing gum importation and sale are banned mainly to keep public spaces clean. While casual possession of small amounts typically doesn't lead to trouble, importing or selling chewing gum illegally can result in **confiscation and fines**. The fines vary but can be several thousand baht depending on the quantity and circumstances. Enforcement tends to focus more on sellers and large-scale importers rather than casual tourists.

- **Unauthorized Drone Use:** Flying drones without official permits is illegal and can lead to **confiscation, fines, or legal action**, especially near sensitive areas.

- **Feeding Stray Animals:** Feeding stray animals is prohibited in some urban areas to control populations and prevent health issues, with **fines or warnings** for offenders.

- **Disrespect Toward Buddhist Monks:** Behaving inappropriately or touching monks, especially by women, is illegal. Because monks hold a highly revered status in Thai society, such actions are taken seriously and offenders may face **warnings, monetary fines, or even arrest** depending on the severity of the offense.

General Questions

1. *How strictly are unusual laws, such as the chewing gum ban or lèse-majesté, enforced on tourists?* The chewing gum ban is generally enforced more against importers and sellers, so casual tourists carrying small amounts usually face minimal issues. However, the lèse-majesté law is enforced very strictly, with serious legal consequences for any perceived insult to the monarchy, regardless of whether the person is a tourist or local.

2. *What penalties can foreigners face if they unknowingly break uncommon or culturally sensitive laws in Thailand?* Foreigners can face **fines, detention, or deportation** even if they unknowingly break laws. Minor offenses might result in warnings or fines, but serious violations—especially those involving the monarchy or public order—can lead to arrest, legal charges, and imprisonment. Ignorance of the law is not usually accepted as a defense.

Law of the Land Hypothetical

HYPOTHETICAL: *Liam, a tourist in Bangkok, finishes chewing a piece of gum and casually sticks it under a public bench instead of disposing of it properly. A local official notices and approaches him. What are the legal consequences of improperly disposing of chewing gum in public places in Thailand?*

ANSWER: *Thailand enforces strict regulations against littering, including the improper disposal of chewing gum, which can result in fines or penalties. Sticking gum under public property is considered littering and disrespectful, and local authorities can impose fines ranging from 1,000 to 5,000 THB (approximately $30 to $150 USD). Repeat offenses may lead to higher fines or community service. Tourists are* *advised to dispose of chewing gum and other trash responsibly in designated bins to avoid fines and show respect for local cleanliness laws.*

CHAPTER 21

TRAVELING SAFELY

IN THIS CHAPTER

- Ladies Traveling Solo
- Traveling as a Family
- Advice for All Travelers
- Do's and Don'ts While in Thailand

TRAVELING SAFELY

Ladies Traveling Solo

Thailand is generally considered a safe and welcoming country for solo female travelers. Millions of women visit each year and enjoy a rich variety of cultural, natural, and culinary experiences without major issues. That said, as with any travel destination, some caution is advised—especially in unfamiliar or nightlife-heavy areas.

While cities like Bangkok, Chiang Mai, and Phuket are usually safe, there are certain neighborhoods and situations where solo women should exercise increased caution. In **Bangkok**, areas such as **Patpong, Nana Plaza**, and **Soi Cowboy**—known for their red-light districts—can become rowdy at night and are best avoided by solo travelers, particularly after dark. In **Pattaya**, the **Walking Street** area can be overwhelming due to its heavy nightlife and alcohol-fueled atmosphere. Solo travelers should also be cautious in isolated beach areas late at night, even in otherwise safe destinations like Phuket, Koh Samui, or Krabi. Outside of major tourist zones, rural or less developed regions may have limited access to emergency services and transportation. Remote stretches of beach or countryside may not be ideal for solo exploration after sundown.

Basic precautions for solo female travelers in Thailand include staying in well-reviewed accommodations, avoiding accepting drinks from strangers, keeping valuables secure, and using trusted transportation options like Grab (the local ride-hailing app) or official taxis. If you plan to go out at night, it's wise to let someone know your plans and avoid walking alone in poorly lit or secluded areas. Dressing modestly in temples or conservative towns, especially in the north or more traditional parts of the country, helps avoid unwanted attention and shows cultural respect. With a mindful approach and basic safety awareness, Thailand can be an incredibly rewarding and secure destination for women traveling alone.

Traveling as a Family

Thailand is widely considered a family-friendly destination, offering a mix of cultural experiences, natural beauty, modern amenities, and activities that appeal to all ages. Whether you're exploring ancient temples, relaxing on a tropical beach, or enjoying vibrant night markets, families with children will find plenty to see and do. Thai people are generally very warm and welcoming toward children, and it's not uncommon for locals to go out of their way to assist families traveling with young ones.

Major tourist cities like Bangkok, Chiang Mai, Phuket, and Krabi are well-equipped with family-oriented accommodations ranging from budget to luxury resorts. Many hotels provide amenities like connecting rooms, family suites, kids' clubs, pools, and even babysitting services. Attractions such as **Siam Ocean World, Dusit Zoo, Chiang Mai Night Safari**, and various water parks and animal sanctuaries provide fun and educational experiences for younger travelers.

Transportation is relatively easy to manage for families. Domestic flights are affordable and convenient, and larger cities have reliable taxis and ride-hailing services. Long-distance train rides can be a comfortable adventure for children, especially with overnight sleeper options. However, it's important for families to plan ahead, especially regarding **food choices, healthcare access**, and **sun protection**. Street food can be delicious but may not always agree with sensitive stomachs, so it's a good idea to start with milder options or eat at places that look clean and busy. Tap water is not drinkable, so bottled water is a must. In terms of safety, Thailand is generally secure, but parents should keep a close eye on children in crowded areas or on beaches with strong currents.

Finally, while Thailand is rich in culture, families should be mindful of customs—such as dressing appropriately at temples and encouraging kids to show respect for Buddhist symbols and statues. With thoughtful planning and cultural awareness, Thailand offers a fantastic, diverse, and memorable travel experience for families.

Advice for All Travelers

While Thailand is a widely visited and generally safe destination, travelers should remain aware and cautious in certain situations to avoid unnecessary risks. Petty theft—such as pickpocketing and bag snatching—can occur, especially in busy markets, tourist hotspots, and on public transport. Always keep your belongings secure and avoid carrying valuables in easily accessible bags. Be wary of common tourist scams, such as tuk-tuk drivers offering "free" tours or individuals claiming that a temple is closed and redirecting you elsewhere for commissions.

It's important to respect local customs and laws, which may differ significantly from those in your home country. Avoid any behavior that could be seen as disrespectful toward the monarchy, religion (especially Buddhism), or cultural norms. Public drunkenness, indecent clothing, and open displays of affection can attract negative attention or legal consequences, particularly in conservative or religious areas.

Use only licensed taxis or rideshare services like **Grab**, and always agree on a fare or ensure the meter is running to avoid overcharging. Be cautious with motorbike rentals—helmets are mandatory, and driving without a valid international license can result in fines or denial of insurance coverage in case of accidents.

Lastly, avoid taking or possessing any form of illegal drugs. Thailand enforces harsh drug laws with severe penalties, including long prison sentences. Even minor offenses can lead to arrest and legal trouble. By staying aware of your surroundings, making informed choices, and respecting local laws and customs, you can enjoy a safe, enjoyable, and respectful trip throughout Thailand.

 **Do's and Don'ts While in Thailand**

Some DO's:

- **DO** dress modestly, especially when visiting religious sites. For both men and women, covering shoulders, chest, and knees is expected in temples (wats). Wearing sleeveless tops, short skirts, or shorts can be considered disrespectful in sacred spaces. Removing shoes before entering someone's home, a temple, or certain shops is also customary.

- **DO** use polite language and tone at all times. Thai culture places a high value on courtesy and self-control. Loud voices, anger, or aggressive behavior can cause offense and rarely lead to a positive outcome.

- **DO** return a "wai" greeting if someone gives you one—especially from someone of similar or older age. While tourists aren't expected to initiate the wai, returning it shows cultural awareness and respect.

- **DO** show respect for monks. Monks are highly revered in Thai society, and certain behaviors are expected around them. For example, women should not touch monks or hand objects directly to them—use a cloth or place the item nearby.

- **DO** carry small change for purchases at street stalls or for tipping service workers. While tipping isn't mandatory, it's appreciated in restaurants, with taxi drivers, hotel porters, and tour guides.

- **DO** learn and use a few basic Thai phrases. Even simple greetings or thank-yous in Thai go a long way in building goodwill with locals. (See Useful Thai Phrases at the end of the book.)

Some DON'Ts:

- **DON'T** criticize or joke about the Thai monarchy, even in private conversations or on social media. Lèse-majesté laws are strict and can result in imprisonment, regardless of nationality.

- **DON'T** touch people on the head. The head is considered the most sacred part of the body in Thai culture, and touching it—even in a friendly manner—can be highly offensive.

- **DON'T** point your feet at people, religious objects, or photos of the royal family. Feet are considered the lowest and "dirtiest" part of the body, symbolically and physically. Avoid placing your feet on tables, chairs, or using them to move objects.

- **DON'T** engage in public displays of affection. While holding hands may be acceptable in some tourist areas, kissing or hugging in public is frowned upon, especially in rural or conservative regions.

- **DON'T** take Buddha images lightly. It's illegal to buy Buddha statues for export without permission, and using Buddha imagery in tattoos or fashion is considered deeply disrespectful.

- **DON'T** touch or take photos of monks without permission, and never climb on statues or ancient ruins for pictures. Many temples have signs reminding visitors of proper conduct—pay attention and follow these guidelines.

CHAPTER 22

TOURIST TAXATION

TOURIST TAXATION

Overview

Tourism plays a vital role in Thailand's economy, contributing significantly to the country's GDP and providing employment across multiple sectors, including hospitality, transportation, food services, and retail. In recent years, tourism has accounted for roughly **10–20% of Thailand's GDP**, depending on the season and global conditions. With millions of visitors each year, the industry generates billions in revenue, supporting both urban development and rural livelihoods. For example, tourism directly contributed about **9%** of Thailand's GDP in 2023, with broader travel & tourism activities accounting for 12% of GDP and over 20% of employment.[34]

Tourists in Thailand are required to pay various taxes, such as VAT (Value-Added Tax) on goods and services, hotel or accommodation taxes, and occasionally entry fees at certain attractions or national parks. These taxes are not arbitrary—they are implemented to ensure that the influx of visitors contributes to the upkeep and improvement of the facilities and services they use. Revenue from tourist taxes is used to maintain infrastructure such as roads, airports, sanitation, and public transport systems. It also supports environmental conservation efforts, particularly in national parks and heritage sites that require careful

---

34 https://tourismanalytics.com/uploads/1/2/0/4/120443739/thai-land-tourism-report-2024.pdf

management due to heavy foot traffic. Additionally, funds are often allocated to healthcare services, public safety, emergency response systems, and tourism promotion. In essence, tourist taxes help make the travel experience safer, cleaner, and more sustainable for both visitors and locals alike.

Tourist Taxes in Thailand

Thailand imposes several types of taxes and fees on tourists to help maintain the infrastructure and services that support the country's booming tourism industry. The main types of tourist-related taxes include the **Value-Added Tax (VAT)**, **accommodation taxes**, and **entry fees** for certain parks and attractions.

The **VAT** in Thailand is set at **7%** and is applied to most goods and services, including dining, shopping, and entertainment. This tax is typically included in the listed price or added at the point of sale. Tourists who make eligible purchases at participating stores can apply for a **VAT refund** at the airport before departure, provided they meet the minimum spending threshold and complete the necessary paperwork.

Hotel and accommodation taxes are generally included in the room rate quoted by hotels, guesthouses, and resorts. These often comprise both the VAT and a local service charge (usually **10%**). The final price you see when booking online or at a hotel counter generally reflects all applicable charges, but it's wise to check. Additionally, there are **entry fees** for national parks, cultural sites, and islands. These fees are higher for foreigners than for Thai nationals and are paid in cash or digitally at the site. For example, visiting a national park may cost a foreigner around **200–400 THB** (approximately **$6-$11 USD**) depending on the location. These taxes are typically **collected automatically through service providers**—such as airlines, hotels, or tour operators—making payment seamless for visitors.

In the future, the Thai government plans to implement a **300 THB tourism fee** (about **$8 USD**) per foreign arrival by air, to be included in ticket prices. This fee is intended to fund tourist insurance, infrastructure upkeep, and emergency services. While it has been delayed, it reflects the broader effort to make tourism more sustainable.[35]

 ## Law of the Land Hypothetical

HYPOTHETICAL: *Elena, a tourist from Spain, purchases several luxury items at a major Bangkok shopping mall. At checkout, she notices a 7% VAT added to her bill. Later, she hears from another traveler that tourists can get a VAT refund before leaving Thailand. Is Elena eligible for a VAT refund, and how can she claim it legally?*

ANSWER: ***Yes***. *Foreign tourists are eligible to receive a VAT refund on qualifying purchases made at participating stores in Thailand. To qualify, the goods must have been purchased at stores displaying a "VAT Refund for Tourists" sign, and the total purchase must amount to at least **2,000 THB (about $55 USD)** per day from a single store. Elena must ask the store for a **PP10 VAT Refund Form** at the time of purchase, and she should keep both the form and her original receipts. Before checking in at the airport on departure, she must present her items, receipts, and passport at the VAT refund inspection counter in the departure hall. After verification, she can submit the documents at the VAT Refund Office in the airport to receive her refund—either in cash (with a small processing fee) or by bank transfer. Failure to follow this process may result in the refund being denied. Therefore, it's important for tourists like Elena to understand the regulations and prepare accordingly if they plan to claim VAT refunds while departing Thailand. For more information, please visit **https://tourist.onesiam.com/en/tax-refunds.***

---

35 https://laotiantimes.com/2025/03/03/
    thailand-to-implement-300-baht-tourism-tax-by-year-end

LONG-TERM STAYS

CHAPTER 23

LONG-TERM STAYS

Overview

Many people choose to stay long-term in Thailand for its combination of **affordability**, **climate**, **lifestyle**, and **accessibility**. Retirees, digital nomads, and expats are drawn to the country's relatively low cost of living, particularly in comparison to Western nations. Cities like Chiang Mai, Bangkok, and coastal areas such as Hua Hin or Phuket offer a diverse range of lifestyles—from quiet and laid-back to fast-paced and urban. Basic expenses like housing, transportation, and food can be managed on modest budgets, with many long-term residents living comfortably on between $1,000 and $2,000 USD per month. In Bangkok, for example, a well-located condo might rent for $400–$700 USD, while meals at local markets often cost just a few dollars. Private healthcare is world-class and reasonably priced, with major hospitals in Bangkok and Chiang Mai often preferred by foreigners for their high standards and English-speaking staff. Although public hospitals are more affordable, the wait times and service quality may not meet the expectations of all foreign residents, making private health insurance or international coverage essential for long-term security.

Thailand's appeal also lies in its culture, natural beauty, and welcoming atmosphere. Long-stay visitors enjoy access to Buddhist temples, tropical beaches, and thriving cultural scenes. **Chiang Mai** has emerged as a hub for digital nomads due to its low costs, coworking spaces, and relaxed pace, while **Bangkok** is ideal for those who want vibrant city life.

Koh Samui, **Phuket**, and **Krabi** are popular among beach lovers and semi-retirees seeking a resort-style existence.

Safety is generally not a concern in most of Thailand. Violent crime is rare, and the country enjoys a reputation for being generally safe for solo travelers and families alike. That said, traffic accidents, scams in tourist areas, and occasional political unrest in Bangkok require awareness. Infrastructure in major cities is modern, with good internet access, hospitals, shopping, and public transport. In rural areas, infrastructure may be less reliable, but community life tends to be more immersive and tranquil.

A significant factor that helps many foreigners settle comfortably in Thailand is the presence of **well-established expat communities**. Bangkok, for instance, hosts a large and diverse group of expats, including professionals, diplomats, entrepreneurs, and retirees. Neighborhoods such as **Sukhumvit** and **Silom** offer international schools, restaurants, and social clubs that cater to foreigners, creating supportive networks for newcomers. Chiang Mai's expat scene is popular among digital nomads and retirees, known for its cozy community feel, frequent social events, and numerous coworking spaces. Coastal towns like Phuket, Pattaya, and Hua Hin attract those who prefer a beach lifestyle, where expat communities often revolve around golf clubs, volunteer activities, and relaxed social gatherings. These communities provide practical help with housing, legal advice, and cultural orientation, while many expats also engage with the local culture by learning Thai and participating in community life, enhancing their long-term experience in the country.

Long-Term Visas[36]

Long-term stays in Thailand are popular among retirees, remote workers, students, and expatriates drawn by the country's rich culture, affordable living costs, and warm climate. Navigating the visa options can be complex, as Thailand offers a variety of visa types tailored to different purposes and durations. Understanding the differences between these

---

36 https://ltr.boi.go.th

visas, their eligibility criteria, and renewal requirements is essential for anyone planning to live in Thailand beyond the typical tourist visit. Here is an overview of the main long-term visa categories and what each entails:

Tourist Visa

The Tourist Visa is the most common initial option for visitors planning shorter stays, typically valid for 60 days and extendable by 30 days at local immigration offices. However, repeated extensions are limited, so it's not designed for long-term residence.

Non-Immigrant Visa

The Non-Immigrant Visa category includes several subtypes tailored to specific purposes:

- The **Non-Immigrant O-A Visa** (**Long Stay**) is for retirees aged 50 and above who meet financial requirements, such as having a bank balance of at least **800,000 THB** (**approximately $23,000 USD**) or a monthly income of at least **65,000 THB** (**around $1,900 USD**). This visa is valid for one year and renewable annually. Applicants must also have health insurance that meets Thai government standards.

- The **Non-Immigrant O Visa** is for those visiting family or volunteering, generally allowing 90-day stays with possible extensions.

- The **Non-Immigrant B Visa** is issued to individuals working in Thailand or conducting business. It requires sponsorship by a Thai employer or company and is usually valid for 90 days initially, with extensions possible up to one year. A work permit is also required to legally work in the country.

- The **Non-Immigrant ED Visa** is intended for students enrolled in recognized educational institutions, including language schools, universities, or professional training courses. It typically allows stays of up to one year, renewable as long as enrollment continues.

Thailand Elite Visa

The Thailand Elite Visa is a special long-term visa program targeting affluent travelers and expatriates. It offers residency privileges ranging from 5 to 20 years, along with VIP services like expedited immigration procedures and airport transfers. Membership fees start at about **600,000 THB (around $17,000 USD)** for the five-year package.

For those wishing to stay beyond the validity of their visa, Thailand's immigration offices allow **visa extensions**, though requirements and fees vary by visa type. Some visas, like the retirement visa, also require periodic health checks and income verification. Foreigners planning to work must secure the proper Non-Immigrant B Visa and obtain a work permit to remain compliant with Thai labor laws.

Navigating visa options can be complex due to changing regulations and documentation requirements. Many long-term residents consult immigration lawyers or visa service agencies to help with applications and renewals. However, despite occasional bureaucracy, Thailand remains a popular destination for long-term living.

 **General Questions**

1. *If I want to stay in Thailand for long-term and work, should I apply for a work permit before arriving in Thailand?* **Yes**. If you plan to work in Thailand long-term, it is advisable to apply for a Non-Immigrant B visa **before** arriving. This visa is required to legally work in Thailand and must be supported by a Thai employer who provides the necessary documentation. Once you enter the country with this visa, you can then apply for a work permit through the Ministry of Labour. Attempting to enter on a tourist visa and switch to a work permit from within Thailand is possible in some cases but often more complicated and not guaranteed to succeed. Securing the proper visa and paperwork in advance is the most reliable and legal route for working in Thailand long-term.

2. *I am American. Can I retire to Thailand?* **Yes**. As an American, you can retire in Thailand through either the **Non-Immigrant O-A (Long Stay)** visa or the **Long-Term Resident (LTR)** visa. The O-A visa is for individuals aged 50+ and allows a one-year stay, renewable annually. To qualify, you must have at least **800,000 THB (about $22,000–$23,000 USD)** in a Thai bank or a monthly income of **65,000 THB (around $1,900 USD)**, plus valid health insurance. The LTR visa, aimed at wealthier retirees, offers a 10-year stay with fewer reporting requirements and the option to bring dependents. Each visa has different benefits, but both are viable paths for Americans seeking to retire long-term in Thailand.

 **Law of the Land Hypothetical**

HYPOTHETICAL: *Mark, a 52-year-old Canadian retiree, moves to Chiang Mai on a 60-day tourist visa, planning to enjoy a quiet lifestyle and affordable living. After signing a one-year condo lease and opening a local bank account, he assumes he can keep extending his tourist visa to stay long-term. Can Mark legally stay in Thailand long-term by continually extending a tourist visa?*

ANSWER: *No. Tourist visas are not meant for long-term residence and can only be extended once or twice. Mark should have applied for a* **Non-Immigrant O-A or O Visa**, *intended for retirees, which requires proof of income or savings, valid health insurance, and typically must be obtained outside Thailand. Overstaying or misusing a tourist visa can result in fines, visa denial, or blacklisting, so long-term visitors must secure the correct visa type to remain legally.*

Takeaways

- Depending on your situation—retirement, work, study, or investment—Thailand provides several visa pathways, including Non-Immigrant O-A (Retirement), B (Business/Work), ED (Education), and the Elite Visa for affluent residents.

- Thailand remains a budget-friendly destination for long-term stays, with monthly living expenses for most foreigners ranging between $1,000 and $2,000 USD, especially outside of Bangkok or in smaller cities like Chiang Mai.

- Major cities offer excellent private medical care at reasonable prices, making health insurance essential but affordable. Long-stay visa holders are often required to show proof of valid health coverage.

- Cities like Bangkok, Chiang Mai, Phuket, and Hua Hin have thriving expat populations that offer newcomers valuable support, from housing tips to visa advice and social networks that ease the transition to life in Thailand.

- Thailand's immigration policies can shift with little notice. Long-term visitors are encouraged to stay informed, maintain required documentation, and consider using visa agents or legal professionals for renewals or more complex applications.

- Foreigners cannot legally work in Thailand without both a valid Non-Immigrant B Visa and an approved work permit. Working on a tourist or retirement visa is illegal and may result in fines, visa cancellation, or deportation.

CIVIL LITIGATION

CIVIL LITIGATION

Overview

Civil litigation provides a mechanism for resolving disputes, ensuring that travelers have a way to seek justice if legal issues arise while visiting another country. It helps them understand their rights and obligations under local laws, which may differ from those in their home country. The civil litigation system offers a formal process for addressing conflicts, such as contract disputes or personal injury claims, and can deter unfair practices by encouraging businesses to comply with legal standards. It also allows individuals to seek financial recourse for damages or losses and helps protect them from potential exploitation by local entities. Overall, understanding civil litigation enhances a visitor's experience and safety while traveling.

Personal Injury Claims and Compensation Law

If a visitor suffers a personal injury while traveling in Thailand—whether due to a traffic accident, a slip and fall in a hotel, an adventure activity gone wrong, or medical negligence—they are legally entitled to pursue compensation under Thai civil law. Personal injury cases in Thailand are governed by the **Civil and Commercial Code**, which allows injured parties to seek financial restitution from the person or entity responsible for the harm. While the process can be more complex for tourists than for residents, legal recourse is still very much available.

The first priority after any injury is to **seek medical attention immediately**. Thailand offers excellent private healthcare services in cities such as Bangkok, Chiang Mai, and Phuket, which are often preferred by foreigners due to higher standards and English-speaking staff. Once stabilized, injured travelers should **report the incident to the police**—particularly if the injury resulted from an accident involving another party. The police report becomes crucial in later legal or insurance proceedings.

Visitors should also document everything related to the incident: photos of the scene, visible injuries, the names and contact information of witnesses, and any official statements or receipts. If the injury occurs in a commercial setting—like a hotel, restaurant, or organized tour—the business may have **liability insurance**, which could cover some or all of the damages. For example, if a tourist slips due to a wet floor with no signage in a resort, the resort may be held liable.

Motorbike and traffic accidents are among the most common causes of injury involving tourists in Thailand. In such cases, Thai law mandates that all drivers carry **compulsory motor insurance**, though coverage levels are often minimal. In serious accidents, the injured party can also sue for damages through the civil court system or negotiate a private settlement, which is common practice in Thailand. However, private settlements, while faster, often involve compromises on the amount of compensation and should be approached carefully—preferably with legal guidance. If a claim proceeds formally, the injured party can pursue **damages for medical costs, loss of income, disability, and pain and suffering**. While Thai courts do not typically award large punitive damages like those in the U.S., they do allow for compensation based on actual financial and physical harm. Emotional distress compensation is possible but is generally modest. The **statute of limitations** for filing a personal injury lawsuit is usually **one year** from the date of the incident.

For tourists with **travel insurance**, the process may be somewhat simpler. Many travel insurance policies cover emergency treatment, hospitalization, evacuation, and sometimes even legal support. However, insurers often place limits on coverage for injuries resulting from risky behavior—such as riding a motorbike without a helmet or license, drinking while operating a vehicle, or engaging in adventure sports without proper supervision. In such cases, coverage could be denied, leaving the traveler to shoulder the costs.

When legal action becomes necessary, foreign claimants can file a lawsuit in Thai civil court but should do so through a **licensed Thai attorney**, as proceedings are conducted in Thai. Some law firms specialize in assisting foreigners and can help with everything from negotiating settlements to courtroom representation. If a settlement is reached outside of court, it must be **written, signed, and witnessed** to be legally binding. This is often preferred when both parties wish to avoid a lengthy court process.

How to File a Civil Claim

Filing a civil claim in Thailand involves a structured legal process governed by the **Thai Civil Procedure Code**. Whether you are a resident or a visitor seeking compensation—for instance, due to personal injury, breach of contract, or property disputes—you must navigate a few key steps to initiate and pursue a claim through the Thai court system.

The process typically begins with **consulting a licensed Thai attorney**, especially important for foreigners, as all court proceedings are conducted in Thai and require formal legal filings. The lawyer will help you assess the merits of your case, gather relevant evidence, and determine the appropriate jurisdiction—usually the court in the province where the incident occurred or where the defendant resides or operates.

Next, your attorney will **draft a formal complaint** detailing the facts of the case, the legal basis for the claim, and the specific remedies or compensation being sought. This complaint is then filed with the appropriate **civil court**, along with the required court fee, which is generally based on the amount of damages claimed (typically around 2% of the claim amount, up to a maximum of 200,000 THB, or $5,400 USD, in most cases). Once the court accepts the claim, the **defendant is served with a summons** and given an opportunity to respond or file a counterclaim. The court will then schedule hearings, which may include attempts at mediation. Thailand strongly encourages out-of-court settlement, and many civil disputes are resolved through this method before proceeding to a full trial. If no settlement is reached, the case moves forward to trial, where both parties present their evidence and witnesses. After reviewing the facts and legal arguments, the judge issues a **verdict**

and judgment, which may include financial compensation, restitution, or other court-ordered remedies. Appeals can be made to a higher court **within 30 days** of the judgment (or 15 days in expedited cases).

Foreigners involved in a civil suit in Thailand must typically appoint a Thai attorney to represent them in court, though in certain small claims cases (under 300,000 THB, or $8,100 USD), representation may not be strictly required. It's also worth noting that **civil judgments in Thailand can be enforced**, including through asset seizure, though the process may take time and additional legal steps.

Overall, filing a civil claim in Thailand is possible for foreigners and visitors, but it demands legal support, proper documentation, and an understanding of the local judicial framework.

Service of Documents[37]

In Thailand, the service of legal documents—such as summonses, complaints, and other court orders—is a formal process governed by the Thai Civil Procedure Code. Unlike in some countries where private process servers can be used, Thailand mandates that **document service be carried out by court officials or appointed officers.** This is to ensure that proper procedure is followed and that all parties receive due notice of legal proceedings.

When a civil or criminal case is filed, the plaintiff must provide the necessary documentation for service, including translations into Thai if the defendant is a foreigner or the documents were originally drafted in another language. The court then assigns a **court officer or bailiff** to physically deliver the documents to the named parties. Personal service—meaning direct hand-delivery—is preferred, and it must be done in a way that guarantees the recipient's awareness of the action against them. However, if the recipient cannot be located or refuses to accept the documents, the officer may leave the documents at the person's residence or workplace, or in certain cases, post a notice on the door. These

---

37 https://lsp-legal.com/lsp-legal/
    international-service-of-process-in-thailand

steps must be documented to demonstrate that reasonable efforts were made to effect service. In some rare situations, the court may permit **service by publication** in a newspaper or other public medium, but this usually applies only when the party's whereabouts are entirely unknown.

For **foreign defendants**, especially in cross-border disputes, service of documents may need to comply with **international treaties** such as the Hague Service Convention, provided both countries are parties to it. However, Thailand is **not a signatory to the Hague Convention**, which can complicate international service and may require diplomatic channels or letters rogatory.

Once service is successfully completed, a **certificate of service** is returned to the court as evidence that proper notice was given. Failing to serve documents properly can result in delays or even dismissal of the case.

Statute of Limitations

In Thailand, the statute of limitations establishes the timeframe within which legal proceedings must be initiated, and it varies depending on the type of case—civil, criminal, labor-related, or administrative. In civil cases, such as breach of contract, the general limitation period is **ten years from the date of breach**, although for specific contract types, like the sale of goods or hire of work, the period may be reduced to two years. **Tort claims**, including those involving personal injury or negligence, must generally be filed **within one year** from the date the injured party becomes aware of both the damage and the identity of the responsible party, with an absolute cutoff at ten years from the incident. **Loan repayment claims** involving a written contract also follow a **ten-year limit**, while claims for **unjust enrichment** must be brought **within one year** from the date the claimant becomes aware of the issue.

Criminal cases in Thailand are subject to varying statutes of limitation depending on the severity of the offense. **Petty offenses** usually have a limitation period of **one year**, while **misdemeanors** that carry sentences of up to one year of imprisonment are subject to a **five-year limitation**. For **felonies** punishable by more than one year and up to seven years, the period extends to **ten years**, and for those exceeding seven years of imprisonment, it increases to **fifteen years**. Crimes that carry life imprisonment have a limitation period of **twenty years**, and **those punishable by death** have **no statute of limitations**, meaning they can be prosecuted at any time. These timeframes generally begin on the date the offense occurred, although they may be paused if the accused flees or hides.

In **labor and employment disputes**, such as wrongful termination, employees typically must file a claim **within two years from the date of the alleged violation. Administrative matters,** including tax disputes, often follow a **five-year limitation** period, although this can extend in cases involving fraud or misrepresentation.

Foreign nationals are subject to the same statutes of limitation as Thai citizens, and cross-border cases may involve international agreements that influence how time limits are calculated. In some civil cases, negotiation or mediation can pause the limitation clock, providing additional time for resolution. Understanding these timeframes is crucial for anyone seeking justice in Thailand, as missing a statutory deadline can permanently bar legal action.

 **Getting Married in Thailand**

Thailand is a popular destination for weddings, particularly for foreign couples seeking a tropical, romantic, and culturally rich setting. Picturesque beaches in Phuket, Krabi, and Koh Samui, serene temples in Chiang Mai, and vibrant city venues in Bangkok make Thailand an attractive choice for destination weddings. In addition to the natural beauty and affordability, the country is known for offering both traditional Thai and Western-style ceremonies, often with experienced planners who help navigate logistics for international guests.

For couples who wish to legally marry in Thailand, there are **specific legal requirements** that must be followed. The process begins with both parties appearing in person at their respective embassies in Bangkok to obtain an **"Affirmation of Freedom to Marry,"** a document stating that each person is legally free to marry. This document must then be translated into Thai and legalized at the Thai Ministry of Foreign Affairs. In addition to this affirmation, foreigners will need their **passports and valid Thai entry stamps**, while Thai nationals will require their ID cards and household registration documents.

There are **legal age requirements** to be aware of—both parties must be **at least 17 years old** (or have parental consent if younger) and not currently married. Polygamy is illegal in Thailand, so any existing marriages must be legally dissolved before registering a new one. Once the required documentation is submitted and approved, the couple may proceed to register the marriage at a local district office (Amphur). This step officially legalizes the marriage under Thai law. There is no mandatory residency period for foreigners, which makes the country especially convenient for destination weddings.

Civil ceremonies in Thailand are purely administrative and conducted at the district office. These are **required for the marriage to be legally recognized. Religious or symbolic ceremonies**—such as traditional Thai weddings or Western-style beach ceremonies—can be held before or after the civil registration but have **no legal status** unless the marriage is officially registered with the government.

The processing time for marriage registration can vary. Obtaining the affirmation from the embassy can often be done in a day or two, while translation and legalization may take another couple of days. The marriage registration at the Amphur office usually takes less than a day once all paperwork is in order. Altogether, couples should allow approximately **4-7 business days** to complete the full legal process. Fees are relatively low: the cost of registering the marriage is minimal (often less than 100 THB or about $3 USD), but services such as translation, legalization, and document processing through agents may add a few hundred to a few thousand baht.

Once registered, the marriage is legally recognized in Thailand, and a Thai marriage certificate is issued. For the marriage to be recognized internationally, couples should have the Thai marriage certificate translated into their home country's language and then legalized at the Ministry of Foreign Affairs. Some countries may also require additional steps for domestic registration back home. Foreign couples are encouraged to check with their embassies or home government offices for country-specific recognition procedures.

 **Law of the Land Hypothetical**

HYPOTHETICAL: *Carlos, a tourist from Spain, was involved in a minor motorbike accident in Bangkok while riding without a helmet. He sustained a concussion but chose not to file a claim or seek immediate legal advice because he thought the injury was minor. After returning to Spain, Carlos begins to experience ongoing headaches, but by the time he decides to take legal action, almost 14 months have passed. Is it too late to file a personal injury lawsuit in Thailand?*

ANSWER: *Yes. Under Thai law, the statute of limitations for personal injury claims is one year from the date of the incident or from when the injured party becomes aware of the damage and the responsible party. Since 14 months have passed since Carlos's accident, he has likely missed the deadline to file a claim in Thai civil court. This one-year limit is strict, and courts usually dismiss cases filed after this period regardless of the circumstances. Exceptions are rare and require extraordinary situations. Carlos's delay in seeking medical or legal advice does not extend this timeframe, and even if he only recently realized the severity of his injury, the limitation period typically does not go beyond one year from awareness. Additionally, because Carlos was riding without a helmet, his travel insurance may deny coverage, making recovery more difficult. As a foreigner, he must follow Thai laws, which take precedence over any home country regulations or treaties. Therefore, it is important for tourists to seek immediate medical attention and legal advice after an injury and to file claims within one year to avoid losing their rights.*

OTHER THINGS TO KNOW

CHAPTER 25

OTHER THINGS TO KNOW

Tourists and Street Hustling

In Thailand, street hustling is a common phenomenon in many tourist-heavy areas, characterized by friendly yet persistent behavior from individuals seeking to engage visitors. These hustlers often approach tourists unsolicited, using high-pressure sales tactics or distractions to lure them into buying goods or services. They may follow tourists or create a sense of urgency to make a quick sale. The goods and services offered range widely but typically include inexpensive jewelry, souvenirs, tuk-tuk or taxi rides, massage services, and sometimes counterfeit or low-quality products. Some hustlers also pose as unofficial tour guides or travel agents, selling fake or overpriced tours and tickets. Tourists should be cautious, as these offers often come with hidden costs or lead to unwanted stops at shops where they may be pressured into buying more expensive items.

Street hustling is most widespread in well-known tourist hotspots like Bangkok's Khao San Road, the bustling streets of Patong Beach in Phuket, Chiang Mai's Night Bazaar, and the lively areas of Pattaya. Common scams include tuk-tuk drivers offering suspiciously cheap tours that inevitably include mandatory stops at jewelry or souvenir shops where tourists are pressured to purchase items. Other scams involve "gem scams," where tourists are sold overpriced or fake gems, and staged distractions such as people asking for help or creating minor accidents to divert attention and steal belongings.

Local authorities and tourism organizations are aware of these issues and take steps to address them through regular police patrols, targeted crackdowns, and public awareness campaigns aimed at educating tourists. Additionally, some areas have introduced official taxi and tour services to provide safer and more reliable options for visitors, although the level of enforcement and effectiveness of these measures can vary depending on the location and time of year.

Safety Concerns and Practical Tips

Interactions with street hustlers in Thailand can sometimes lead to safety concerns such as petty theft, scams, or harassment. Aggressive hustlers may pressure tourists into buying unwanted goods or services, and in some cases, distractions created during these encounters can lead to pickpocketing or loss of belongings. There is also the risk of verbal confrontations or feeling unease if a tourist refuses to engage or pay.

To protect themselves, tourists should remain polite but firm in declining unsolicited offers and avoid getting drawn into long conversations or negotiations on the street. It's wise to keep valuables secure and be cautious when approached by strangers, especially in crowded or tourist-heavy areas. Using reputable and official services for taxis, tours, and massages can reduce the risk of scams. Trusting your instincts and walking away from any situation that feels uncomfortable is important.

Understanding local customs can also help tourists navigate street interactions more safely. For example, a polite but clear "no, thank you" is usually respected, and avoiding direct confrontation helps keep the situation calm. Tourists can report harassment or scams to local police stations, or through tourist police, who are often stationed in major tourist areas and speak English. Many cities also have tourism help centers or hotlines where visitors can seek assistance if they encounter problems related to street hustlers.

 ## In the Event of Death

If a death occurs in Thailand, it is crucial to act promptly by notifying the local authorities. The first point of contact should be the local police and the nearest hospital or medical facility. The police will conduct an official investigation, especially if the death is sudden, unexpected, or suspicious, and will issue a death certificate, which is a vital document for all subsequent legal and administrative procedures. If the death occurs in a hospital, medical staff will assist in notifying the authorities and issuing necessary medical reports. It's important for family or traveling companions to gather and secure the deceased's personal documents, such as passport and identification cards, as these will be needed throughout the process.

Once local authorities are informed, contacting your country's embassy or consulate is essential. Embassies can provide crucial support by advising on legal requirements, assisting with documentation, and acting as a liaison between the family and Thai officials. They can also help in notifying next of kin if they haven't been informed. The embassy will typically require several documents, including the official death certificate, passport of the deceased, police and medical reports, and proof of relationship from the next of kin. They may also provide guidance on funeral arrangements and repatriation options. If the family wishes to bring the body back home, the embassy can assist in coordinating with local funeral homes and airlines to ensure proper handling according to international regulations.

Dealing with a death abroad can be emotionally and logistically challenging, so it's important for family members or companions to stay in close contact with both local officials and their embassy. Funeral arrangements in Thailand can vary from simple cremations to more elaborate ceremonies depending on local customs and family wishes. Some families may choose to conduct the funeral locally, while others opt for repatriation. Throughout this process, maintaining clear communication and seeking help from professional services—such as funeral directors experienced in handling foreign cases—can help ease the burden. Additionally, embassies often provide lists of local legal representatives, translators, and counseling services to support grieving families during this difficult time.

Experiencing Financial Hardship

Tourists visiting Thailand may experience financial hardship for several reasons. Common causes include unexpected medical emergencies, theft or loss of wallets and passports, sudden changes in travel plans such as flight cancellations, or underestimating daily expenses and overspending. Some travelers may also face difficulties due to currency exchange issues or scams that drain their funds. Additionally, unforeseen events like natural disasters or political unrest can disrupt travel plans and cause financial strain.

If tourists run out of money or need financial assistance while in Thailand, they should immediately reach out to their country's embassy or consulate. Embassies often provide emergency assistance, such as helping to arrange funds through family or friends back home or guiding travelers to local support services. It's also advisable to reach out to one's travel insurance provider if coverage is in place, as some policies include emergency financial aid or repatriation support. Travelers should avoid borrowing money from strangers or unverified sources to reduce the risk of falling victim to scams.

To manage expenses effectively and avoid financial hardship, tourists should familiarize themselves with local costs and currency before and during their trip. The Thai baht (THB) is the official currency, and understanding exchange rates and typical prices for food, transportation, and accommodations can help travelers budget appropriately. Many areas in Thailand accept cash, but credit cards are widely used in cities and tourist spots. Using trusted money exchange services and avoiding street exchangers can prevent losses. Additionally, setting daily spending limits and tracking expenses can help maintain control over finances throughout the visit.

QUICK REFERENCE GUIDE

▪ Quick Chapter References to Important Topics

QUICK REFERENCE GUIDE

Crime in Thailand

Are there particular areas I should avoid as a tourist?

Yes. Thailand is generally safe for tourists, but it's wise to avoid the **Deep South provinces** like **Pattani**, **Yala**, and **Narathiwat** due to ongoing insurgent violence. Some remote border **areas near Myanmar** may also pose risks due to occasional conflict or instability. Exercise caution in **red-light districts** such as **Patpong** or **Nana Plaza** in Bangkok and **Walking Street** in Pattaya, where scams and petty crime are more common. It's also best to steer clear of political protests, isolated beaches at night, and unregulated adventure activities. Sticking to well-traveled areas and using common sense will help ensure a safe and enjoyable trip. *For more details, see Chapter 3.*

Drug Offenses

Is the possession of marijuana legal?

No. Recreational marijuana is **illegal** in Thailand, and tourists are not permitted to buy, possess, or use cannabis without a valid Thai-issued medical prescription. **Medical cannabis** is **allowed only under strict regulation**: a licensed Thai physician, dentist, pharmacist, or certified traditional medicine practitioner must issue a prescription, which typically covers a maximum 30 day supply and must specify dosage and condition. Tourists can legally access medical cannabis only if they obtain this prescription in Thailand; foreign prescriptions are not recognized, and cannabis must be bought from licensed dispensaries sourcing GACP certified products. Public consumption is prohibited and can lead to **fines up to 25,000 THB (about $772 USD) or imprisonment under the Public Health Act.**

Is the possession of cocaine legal?

No. Possession of cocaine is **illegal** in Thailand and carries severe penalties. Even small amounts can result in up to 5 years in prison and fines of up to **100,000 THB (about $2,900 USD).** Larger quantities or intent to distribute can lead to life imprisonment or even the death penalty. There are no exceptions for tourists—foreigners face full prosecution and may also be deported. *For more details, see Chapter 4.*

Alcohol-Related Offenses

What is the legal drinking age?

The legal drinking age in Thailand is **20 years old.** This applies to both purchasing and consuming alcoholic beverages. The law is enforced for both locals and foreigners, regardless of the legal drinking age in their home countries. While some establishments may not always check IDs, underage drinking is illegal and can result in fines or other penalties. It's important to adhere to this regulation to avoid legal issues during your visit.

What is the legal blood alcohol limit to drive?

In Thailand, the legal blood alcohol concentration (BAC) limit for drivers is **0.05%** (50 milligrams of alcohol per 100 milliliters of blood). For **drivers under 20 years old**, the limit is stricter at **0.02%** (20 mg/100 ml). **Commercial and professional drivers** are also subject to the **0.02%** limit. If a driver refuses a breathalyzer test, it is assumed they have exceeded the legal limit, and penalties apply accordingly. Penalties for drunk driving can include fines, imprisonment, and license suspension, with severity increasing for repeat offenders or if the driver causes injury or death. *For more details, see Chapter 5.*

Firearm & Ammunition Offenses

Can I possess a gun?

No. Tourists cannot legally possess firearms in Thailand. Gun ownership is restricted to Thai citizens under strict laws. While foreigners may use licensed shooting ranges for controlled activities, carrying or owning a gun without proper authorization can lead to severe penalties, including imprisonment and fines.

Can I possess ammunition?

No. As a tourist, you **cannot legally possess ammunition in Thailand**. Thai law prohibits foreigners from owning firearms and ammunition, regardless of whether they are in the country temporarily or permanently. Possessing ammunition without a valid firearm license is a criminal offense. Attempting to bring ammunition into Thailand, even in small quantities, is illegal and can lead to severe legal consequences. *For more details, see Chapter 6.*

Prostitution

Is prostitution legal?

No. Prostitution in Thailand is technically **illegal under laws that ban solicitation, brothel operation, and pimping**, though the exchange of sex for money itself is not explicitly outlawed. Despite this, sex work is widespread and often tolerated in certain areas. Recent proposals aim to decriminalize and regulate the industry, but for now, tourists should know that engaging in prostitution carries legal risks and could lead to fines or arrest. *For more details, see Chapter 7.*

LGBTQ

Is homosexuality legal?

Yes. Homosexuality is **legal** in Thailand. Same-sex sexual activity has been legal since 1956, and the age of consent has been equalized since 1997. In January 2025, Thailand became the first country in Southeast Asia to legalize same-sex marriage, granting same-sex couples the same legal rights as heterosexual couples, including adoption rights . Public opinion in Thailand is largely supportive, with surveys indicating high levels of acceptance and support for same-sex marriage . While societal attitudes are generally positive, challenges remain in areas such as gender recognition and comprehensive anti-discrimination protections.

Are same-sex public displays of affection legal?

Yes. However, while homosexuality is legal in Thailand, public displays of affection (PDA), including those by same-sex couples, are **generally discouraged** due to cultural norms valuing modesty and privacy. Holding hands is increasingly accepted in urban areas like Bangkok, especially among LGBTQ+ couples, but public kissing remains rare and may attract attention. In more rural regions, such displays can be viewed as inappropriate. Therefore, while not illegal, it's advisable for LGBTQ+ visitors to exercise discretion and reserve intimate gestures for private settings to align with local customs and avoid unwanted attention. *For more details, see Chapter 8.*

Arrested in Thailand

Would I be entitled to bail if I'm arrested?

If you are arrested in Thailand, you are **generally entitled to bail**, but it is **not automatic**. The court decides whether to grant bail based on factors such as the severity of the offense, risk of flight, and potential interference with the investigation. For minor offenses, bail is more commonly granted, often with conditions. However, for serious crimes, especially those involving drugs or violence, bail may be denied. It's important for foreigners to seek legal assistance promptly to navigate the bail process.

Will a lawyer be provided to me if I cannot afford one?

In Thailand, if you cannot afford a lawyer, you **may be eligible for legal aid** through government or non-profit legal assistance programs. However, **free legal representation is not guaranteed** for all cases, and the availability of public defenders is limited compared to some other countries. Foreigners are strongly advised to hire a private attorney whenever possible, as navigating the Thai legal system can be complex and language barriers can pose challenges. *For more details, see Chapter 10.*

Helping a Friend or Relative Imprisoned in Thailand

Can I send money to a friend or relative imprisoned in Thailand?

Yes. You can send money to a friend or family member imprisoned in Thailand by depositing funds into their prison account, which they use to buy approved items. Deposits can be made in person during visiting hours or at certain bank branches like Krung Thai Bank, though availability varies by prison. It's best to contact the specific prison or the Department of Corrections for details on how to send money.

Can I remain in the country upon release from prison or jail after my sentence is complete?

After completing a prison sentence in Thailand, your ability to remain in the country depends on your visa status. If your visa has expired or is about to expire, you may be required to leave. Immigration authorities may also review your case, especially if your conviction involved serious crimes. In some situations, you might face deportation or a ban on re-entry. It's important to check with immigration officials and possibly seek legal advice to understand your options for staying in Thailand after release. *For more details, see Chapter 12.*

Crime Victim Assistance

Can a victim of a crime be legally compensated?

Yes. Victims of crimes in Thailand can seek legal compensation through civil litigation. If the crime caused personal injury or financial loss, the victim can file a civil claim against the offender to recover damages for medical costs, lost income, and other harms. Compensation claims are separate from criminal proceedings and must be pursued within the statute of limitations, typically one year for personal injury cases. It's advisable for victims to consult a Thai attorney to navigate the process effectively.

Does the Thailand government offer assistance for family members of homicide victims?

Yes. The Thai government provides assistance to family members of homicide victims through the Victim Compensation and Restitution Board, which offers financial support for funeral and related expenses. The Ministry of Social Development and Human Security also provides counseling and legal aid. While support is available, navigating the process can be complex, so seeking help from legal professionals or victim support groups is recommended. *For more details, see Chapter 14.*

U.S. Consulate Assistance

Are there any limitations to the consulate assistance I can receive while in Thailand?

Yes. Consulate assistance in Thailand is helpful but limited. Consulates can provide support such as helping with lost passports, notifying family, and offering lists of local lawyers or medical services. However, they cannot intervene in legal matters, pay fines, or secure your release from jail. They also cannot provide financial aid or act as your personal attorney. It's important to understand these limits and seek local legal help if needed. *For more details, see Chapter 14.*

Police

Is there an official police force?

Yes. Thailand has an official national police force called the Royal Thai Police. They are responsible for maintaining law and order, investigating crimes, and ensuring public safety throughout the country. *For more details, see Chapter 15.*

How to Get Legal Help in Thailand

Is there a resource in Thailand to find legal representation?

Yes. Thailand has resources to help you find legal representation. The Thai Bar Association provides referrals to licensed attorneys, and there are also law firms specializing in assisting foreigners. Consulting these resources can help you find qualified legal help.

Is there free legal representation assistance?

Yes. Free legal representation is available in Thailand mainly through the Thai Bar Association, which offers pro bono services to low-income individuals. The Office of the Attorney General, the Court of Justice, and university legal aid centers like Chulalongkorn University also provide free legal advice and assistance. For foreigners, some law firms offer free initial consultations, but full representation may involve fees. Availability and scope can be limited, so it's best to contact these organizations directly to check eligibility and services.

Does my home country's embassy provide a list of local attorneys who speak English?

Yes. Many foreign embassies in Thailand provide lists of local attorneys who speak English to assist their citizens. These lists typically include lawyers experienced in helping foreigners with legal issues in Thailand. It's a good idea to contact your embassy directly for their recommended legal contacts. *For more details, see Chapter 16.*

Foreign Embassies in Thailand

Are there foreign embassies in Thailand?

Yes. Thailand hosts many foreign embassies, primarily located in Bangkok. These embassies provide services such as passport renewal, emergency assistance, and legal or medical referrals for their citizens. If you're traveling or living in Thailand, it's a good idea to know where your country's embassy is and how to contact it in case of emergencies.

Is there a website to locate embassies in Thailand?

> **Yes.** You can locate diplomatic missions in Thailand at **https://www. embassy-worldwide.com/country/thailand**. This site includes a full directory of foreign embassies and consulates in Thailand, complete with contact details and locations. You can also check your own country's foreign affairs website, which often lists its overseas embassies, including those in Thailand. *For more details, see Chapter 16.*

Medical Facilities & Hospitals

What is the number I can call for ambulance and fire emergencies?

> You can call **1669** for **ambulance and medical emergencies** and **199** for **fire emergencies**. These are nationwide emergency numbers and are generally reachable 24/7. English-speaking operators may be available, especially in major cities and tourist areas.

If I am injured while on vacation in Thailand, are there hospitals that are recommended for tourists?

> **Yes.** If you're injured while on vacation in Thailand, there are several hospitals recommended for tourists, especially in major cities. Top facilities like **Bumrungrad International Hospital, Bangkok Hospital**, and **Samitivej Hospital** in Bangkok offer high-quality care, English-speaking staff, and experience handling international patients. Similar standards can be found in popular destinations like Phuket and Chiang Mai. Many of these hospitals also assist with insurance and translation services. *For more details, see Chapter 17.*

Driving in Thailand

Which side of the road do I drive on?

> In Thailand, you drive on the **left-hand side** of the road. This means the steering wheel is typically on the right side of the vehicle. If you're renting a car, be sure you're comfortable with this setup and local traffic laws, as driving customs can differ from what you're used to.

Can I use my driver's license from my home country to drive in Thailand?

Yes. You can drive in Thailand using your home country's driver's license **only if it is accompanied by a valid International Driving Permit** (**IDP**). The IDP must be obtained in your home country before arrival. Without it, your foreign license alone may not be legally accepted, and you could face fines or be denied insurance coverage in case of an accident.

How old do I need to be to rent a car?

To rent a car in Thailand, you generally need to be **at least 21 years old** and have held a valid driver's license for at least one year. Some rental companies may require drivers to be 23 or older, and drivers under 25 may face a young driver surcharge. An International Driving Permit is also typically required for foreigners. *For more details, see Chapter 18.*

Nude Beaches & Clothing-Optional Resorts

Is public nudity legal on the beaches?

No. Public nudity is not legal on beaches in Thailand. It is considered indecent and can lead to fines, arrest, or other legal consequences. While some tourists may sunbathe topless in certain areas, especially on remote beaches, it is generally frowned upon and not culturally acceptable. It's best to dress modestly and respect local norms. *For more details, see Chapter 19.*

Tourist Taxation

Is there room tax in Thailand?

Yes. Thailand imposes a **room tax** on hotel stays, typically included in the price. This often consists of a **7% value-added tax** (**VAT**) and, in some cases, an additional **service charge of around 10%**. Some hotels may also include a **1% provincial or local tax**. Always check your bill, as these charges are usually itemized at checkout.

Is there any fee associated with leaving Thailand?

Yes. There is a departure fee when leaving Thailand, but it's usually included in your airline ticket price. For international flights, the fee is about 730 baht (as of April 2024) and applies at major airports like Bangkok, Phuket, and Chiang Mai. For domestic flights, the fee is around 130 baht. No separate payment is needed at the airport. *For more details, see Chapter 22.*

Long-Term Stays

Do I need to return to my home country to apply for a work permit in Thailand?

No. You don't need to return to your home country to apply for a work permit in Thailand. However, you must first get a Non-Immigrant B Visa (usually from a Thai embassy abroad) before entering Thailand. Once in Thailand, your employer can help you apply for the work permit locally.

As an American, how long can I stay in Thailand without a visa?

As an American, you can stay in Thailand **visa-free for up to 60 days** if arriving by air, with the option to extend your stay by 30 days at an immigration office, totaling 90 days. If entering via land or sea, the visa-free stay is 30 days, limited to two entries per year. Be sure to complete the Thailand Digital Arrival Card before arrival and avoid overstaying to prevent fines or deportation. *For more details, see Chapter 23.*

In the Event of Death

What documents would an embassy need regarding the death of a tourist?

For the death of a tourist, an embassy typically requires a death certificate issued by local authorities, the deceased's passport or ID, a police report or investigation report if applicable, and a medical or hospital report confirming the cause of death. They may also ask for proof of relationship from the next of kin to assist with communication and support, as well as details about funeral or re-patriation arrangements if needed. These documents help the embassy provide assistance and handle necessary legal and logistical matters. *For more details, see Chapter 25.*

EMERGENCY/IMPORTANT CONTACT NUMBERS IN THAILAND

 Please consider putting some of these numbers in your phone **prior** to traveling to Thailand.

Emergency Numbers:

- **Police:** 191
- **Fire Department:** 199
- **Ambulance & Rescue Services:** 1669

Other Useful Contacts:

- **Tourist Police (English-speaking):** 1155
- **Coast Guard:** 1584
- **Roadside Assistance (Department of Land Transport):** 1193
- **General Emergency Services:** 1669

Legal Assistance:

Thai Bar Association (Lawyers Council of Thailand)
Phone: +66 2 620 6666
Website: www.lawyerscouncil.or.th

Ministry of Justice (Legal Aid Office)
Phone: +66 2 141 5800
Website: www.moj.go.th

Office of the Attorney General (Legal Aid)
Phone: +66 2 141 9000 (main office)
Email: lawaid@ago.go.th
Website: www.ago.go.th

USEFUL THAI PHRASES

Greetings

HI/HELLO – สวัสดี (sa-wat-dee)

GOOD MORNING – สวัสดีตอนเช้า (sa-wat-dee ton chao)

GOOD AFTERNOON – สวัสดีตอนบ่าย (sa-wat-dee ton bai)

GOOD NIGHT – ราตรีสวัสดิ์ (raa-tree sa-wat)

GOODBYE – ลาก่อน (laa-gorn)

Magic Words

PLEASE – กรุณา (ka-ru-naa)

THANK YOU – ขอบคุณ (khop-khun)

YOU'RE WELCOME – ยินดีครับ/ค่ะ (yin-dee khráp/kâ)

CHEERS! – ชนแก้ว! (chon-gaew!)

EXCUSE ME – ขอโทษครับ/ค่ะ (khor-thôt khráp/kâ)

Getting Around

WHERE IS THE BATHROOM? – ห้องน้ำอยู่ที่ไหน? (hông-nám yùu thîi năi?)

WHAT TIME IS IT? – ตอนนี้เวลาเท่าไหร่? (ton-níi wee-laa thâo-rài?)

HOW DO I GET TO...? – ไป...อย่างไร? (bpai... yàang-rai?)

WHERE DOES THIS TRAIN/BUS GO? – รถไฟ/รถบัสนี้ไปไหน? (rót-fai/rót-bát níi bpai năi?)

RESTAURANT – ร้านอาหาร (ráan aa-hăan)

HOW MUCH DOES THIS COST? – ราคาเท่าไหร่? (raa-khaa thâo-rài?)

TRAIN/METRO STATION – สถานีรถไฟ/รถไฟฟ้า (sà-thăa-nii rót-fai / rót-fai-fáa)

Communication

Emergency

GLOSSARY

ACQUITTAL: A jury verdict that a criminal defendant is not guilty, or the finding of a judge that the evidence cannot support a conviction.

ADVERSARY PROCEEDING: A lawsuit arising from a controversy that begins with filing a complaint.

AFFIDAVIT: A written statement made under oath.

APPEAL: A request made after a trial court has decided against one party in which the losing party asks a higher court to review the decision for legal error.

ARRAIGNMENT: A proceeding in which a criminal defendant is brought to court, told of the charges, and asked to plead guilty or not guilty.

BAIL: The temporary release of a person from jail when awaiting trial, on condition that a sum of money be lodged or deposited to guarantee an appearance in court.

BARRISTER: A lawyer admitted to plead at the Bar and who may try cases in superior court.

BURDEN OF PROOF: The duty to prove disputed facts.

CAUSE OF ACTION: A legal claim in a civil action.

COMPLAINT: A written statement that begins a civil lawsuit in which the plaintiff details the claims.

CONTRACT: An agreement between two or more persons to do something or to not do something.

CONVICTION: A judgment of guilt against a person charged with a crime.

CUSTOMS DUTY: A tariff or tax imposed on goods when transported across international borders.

COURT LIAISON: A person that coordinates with attorneys to perform administrative duties, such as scheduling witnesses, sharing information with law enforcement, and overseeing the reporting of cases to foreign embassies when applicable.

DAMAGES: Money that a defendant pays to a plaintiff in a civil case if the plaintiff wins.

DEFENDANT: 1) The individual against whom a civil claim is filed; 2) The individual against whom a criminal claim is filed.

FELONY: A serious crime, punishable by more than one year in prison.

MAGISTRATE: A judicial officer of a district court, who conducts initial proceedings in criminal cases, decides criminal misdemeanor cases, conducts many pretrial civil and criminal matters on behalf of district judges, and decides civil cases with the consent of the parties.

MISDEMEANOR: An offense punishable by one year or less in jail.

PLAINTIFF: A person or business that files a formal complaint with the court.

PLEA: In a criminal case, the answer of "guilty," "not guilty," or "no contest" in response to a criminal charge.

SOLICITOR: A lawyer who advises clients, represents them in lower court, and prepares cases for barristers to try in higher courts.

SOVEREIGN IMMUNITY: A legal doctrine by which the sovereign or the state (i.e. government) cannot commit a legal wrong and thus, it is immune from criminal and civil liability and cannot be sued.

STATUTE: A written law passed by a legislative body.

STATUTE OF LIMITATIONS: A statute prescribing a period of limitation to bring certain types of legal actions. If the action is not brought within that time, the person or entity (in a criminal context) is permanently barred from suing in court.

SUBPOENA: A command, issued under court authority, for a witness to appear and to give testimony.

TESTIMONY: Evidence presented orally by witnesses.

VERDICT: The decision of a judge or jury in a case.

WARRANT: Court authorization to conduct a search or to make an arrest.

ACKNOWLEDGMENTS

This book series would never have seen the light of day without the able assistance of the following people:

Kathy Adams, my paralegal for over 22 years, who is the "Best" I've ever worked with during my entire legal career because of her amazing work ethic, organizational skills, and her ability to think outside of the box in unique and creative ways;

Ally Knez-Siddique, a professional writer, and one of my paralegals, whose eye for detail, according to her, is both a blessing and a curse;

Gino Ibanez, my former law clerk, whose exceptional research skills helped move this book series along in its early stages;

Rosa Diaz Graham, my legal assistant who helped with research and word processing at the very beginning of this project;

Shelia Martin, one of my former paralegals, worked diligently on this series of books, even after taking on another job. Her organizational skills are reflected throughout;

Mindy Scarlett, my marketing and publishing "Guru"! Her creativity and vision have no boundaries!

ABOUT THE AUTHOR

Michael L. Moore practices in Orlando, Florida, the city where he spent his formative years. He credits the trauma of having his brother murdered when he was only 10 years old, as the catalyst that drew him into the practice of law.

Moore attended Florida State University, where he was a member of the FSU debate team. Upon graduating, he was awarded a full scholarship to attend the University of Tennessee College of Law, where he was elected President of the Student Bar Association. He further honed his advocacy and public speaking skills by participating in 'moot court' competitions.

After clerking at the Tennessee Attorney General's office while in law school, Moore moved back to Orlando, Florida, to work at the State Attorney's Office as a prosecutor, and where he was fortunate enough to meet the young lady that would eventually become his wife. Moore moved on to working for private law firms, both local and national, and eventually established his own law firm in 1999. He continues to make Orlando his home base.

It was the murder of a close friend and client in Jamaica that caused Moore to realize that books on laws in other countries were few and far between, and he was inspired to create Law of the Land Publishing. Moore launched Law of the Land Publishing to provide a series of guidebooks and a membership site for tourists and business travelers to stay up to date on the laws in each country they travel to, as well as having access to assistance if they run into legal issues.

"My vision is to educate people on what their legal rights are, and how they can access legal assistance, no matter where they have to travel to in the world," said Moore. "As Americans, we have a right to due process, but in some countries, you don't even have the right to access a square meal when incarcerated. My goal is to provide the information needed to stay out of trouble, as well as having access to assistance if trouble finds you."

www.ingramcontent.com/pod-product-compliance
Lightning Source LLC
Chambersburg PA
CBHW071722120626
46550CB00001B/344